HARMONY

A PROGRESSIVE LOOK AT MUSIC THEORY

BY BRENDA HAYWARD

HARMONY
A PROGRESSIVE LOOK AT MUSIC THEORY

Published by Music Maker Books Ltd, Alexander House, Forehill, Ely
Cambs., CB7 4AF, England.
© Brenda Hayward 1993
ISBN: 1 870951 14 X

Edited and produced by Penny Braybrooke

Designed by Rob Berry

Printed by Caligraving Limited, Thetford

■ FOREWORD

It may be a cliche but Brenda Hayward really needs no introduction; for thousands of people she has been the inspiration behind their learning to play the keyboard. Whether they be raw beginners or those searching for the key to the next step up the ladder, Brenda has been able to give help and guidance through her books, magazine articles and seminars.

How does she do it? Well, her plain speaking - whether on the page or in person at festivals and her own Harmony Wise Weekends - cuts through the pomposity and mystique often used by experts. She approaches her subject with clarity and an understanding of her pupils' needs built up over years of talking to and aiding amateur players - she is no stuffy musicologist concerned merely with the rules of music.

Those who have met Brenda will know she is a warm and understanding person. Many is the time I have seen her late for meals and her own well-deserved bedtime at festivals because she is patiently explaining the finer points of the 'Circle of Fifths' or other such element of theory to avid enthusiasts who see no dividing line between her on and off duty hours. Indeed, she has no such terms herself, and despite these pressures on her own leisure time she still has an empathy with all those who seek her expert help.

This book will help anyone groping in the dark for a light to lead them through the murky tunnels of music theory. Brenda Hayward is that light.

Malcolm Harrison
Editor, 'Keyboard Review'

■ CONTENTS

PART II   *Harmony*

PART III   *The Professional Touch*

PART I

PRELUDE TO HARMONY

For initial registration use flute voices: on an organ, for instance, the 8ft flute plus sustain for the pedals and a good balance of sounds with the upper manual voices slightly louder than the lower manual on a dual manual organ. Use the voices with discretion, too few rather than too many.

The keys will sustain and continue to sound while being held and the technique for playing the melody is to allow the fingers to crawl from one note to the next, releasing each note at the last moment before playing the next note to create the sustained organ sound. 'Linger a little longer on each note' should be the initial rule.

The left hand will feel strange at first because of its playing position and playing action to create the sustained left hand chords. The left hand will be held (sustained) on the manual and when changing from one chord to the next, finger movement only will achieve smooth chord changing sequences. On a dual manual organ, every chord except thirteenths should be played between the octave F to F either side of middle C on the lower manual. Explanations and illustrations throughout this book show how this is achieved by using chord inversions. This playing position allows the sound of the left hand chord to be separated from the deep bass pedal notes in the same way that the melody, although blending with the chords, is a separately heard sound.

Bass pedals are played with the toe of the left foot and provide a beautifully deep bass sound to the music. It is most important that from the beginning the bass pedal note is played at the same time as the left hand chord. The foot pedal on the right of the organ is the overall volume control and is also used to give expression to your playing by carefully controlled use. The expression pedal should never be pumped up and down to the rhythm of the music.

Develop all the playing skills within your ability to create the richness and beauty of sound that the modern electronic organ is capable of producing and even though you are a solo performer, you can begin to sound like a full orchestra.

Registration has not been suggested for the arrangements featured later in the book as the sound you would like to hear is a personal choice. However, most electronic organs have an owners manual or registration chart included in the 'Bench Pack', to show the correct set up for the organ voices.

■ THE KEYBOARD MANUAL

Black and white notes form repetitive patterns on the manual. The name of each white note is represented by a letter of the alphabet from A to G (A B C D E F G). This sequence of note names is repeated the full length of the keyboard, for example on a dual manual organ the notes are:

Upper manual

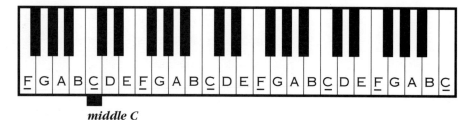

middle C

Lower manual

middle C

The black notes are arranged in groups of two and three. The notes of C, which are underlined, are located to the left of any two black notes and the notes of F, also underlined, are located to the left of any three black notes. The manual illustrations in this book start on the note of F but, as keyboard manuals vary in length, they can start on other notes.

■ READING A MANUSCRIPT

A manuscript consists of a treble and possibly a bass stave. The treble stave starts with a treble clef sign

The bass stave starts with a bass clef sign

𝄢

The lines and spaces of the treble stave are: E F G A B C D E F.

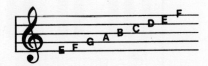

And those of the bass stave are: G A B C D E F G A.

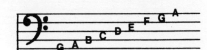

Notice how the names of the treble and bass staves differ. The first line of the treble stave is E while the first line of the bass stave is G.

Treble & bass staves joined on the manuscript

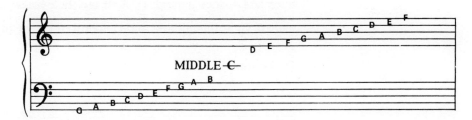

Middle C appears on a short line between the two staves, known as a ledger line.

On a two manual organ, melody notes written on the treble stave are played with the right hand on the upper manual. Groups of notes written on the bass stave are played as left hand chords on the lower manual.

The treble & bass staves in relation to the organ manuals.

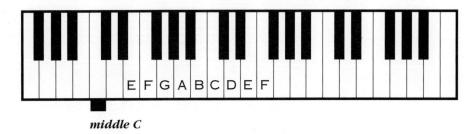

middle C

Upper manual for playing the melody

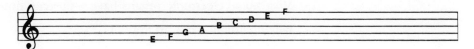

Right hand

Lower manual for playing chords

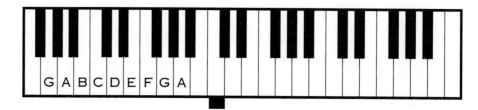

middle C

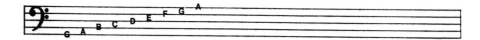

Left hand

The notes on both staves follow an alphabetical sequence from A to G. Ledger lines are used on the manuscript when the notes are too high or too low to be written on the staves but the notes will maintain the alphabetical sequence when ascending. Above the treble staves are additional ledger lines and spaces named; G, A, B etc. Below the treble stave, the notes are named; G, A, B, middle C and D, followed by the first line of E.

Treble stave

Above the bass stave are the notes of B, middle C, D, E etc., while below the bass stave C, D, E and F precede the first line of G.

Bass stave

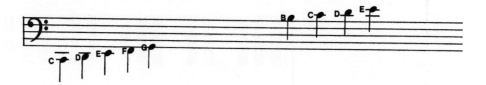

There are two E and F notes on the treble stave and two G and A notes on the bass stave.

■ THE BASS PEDALS

Most home electronic organs have a thirteen note pedal board, with notes ranging from lower C to upper C.

Thirteen note pedal board shown in relation to the bass stave

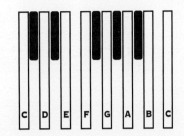

The left foot is used to play the bass pedals, which combine with the left hand playing chords and the right hand playing the melody, to create the full rich sound of the electronic organ. The pedal board note names are identical to the note names on the organ manuals. The lower C note is to the left of two black notes and the F note is to the left of the three black notes.

■ USING THE EXPRESSION PEDAL

On a dual manual organ the expression pedal, to the right of the pedal board, controls the volume. It should be used to emphasise phrases of music to give expression to your playing. Always rest your right foot upon this pedal for a comfortable body balance, but do not beat time with the expression pedal by moving it up and down to the rhythm of the music.

■ FINGERING

To avoid a common problem of incorrect fingering when playing a keyboard, identify the thumb as number 1, the little finger as number 5 and the remaining fingers as numbers 2, 3 and 4 on each hand.

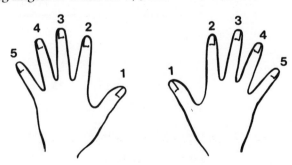

Try to play the upward sequence of notes on the treble stave in the following illustration. Using the right hand, the thumb (1) plays G, followed by fingers 2 and 3 playing the A and B. Tuck your thumb underneath the hand to play the next highest note of the music, C, before dropping fingers 2 and 3 onto the next two notes of D and E on the upper manual.

Fingering

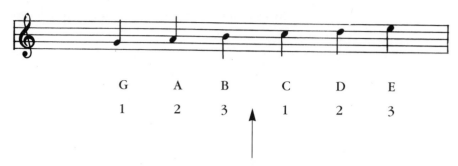

G	A	B		C	D	E
1	2	3		1	2	3

Tuck thumb under the hand

To ensure that you are seated comfortably at the organ, sit opposite the middle C note.

■ SHARPS & FLATS

When a note is raised or lowered it is said to be sharpened or flattened.

The short black notes on keyboard manuals and organ pedal boards are sharpened and flattened white notes. To sharpen a note means that its pitch, or sound, is raised by movement to the next higher note on its right, ie. play the note of A followed by the black note on its immediate right. This black note is A sharp (A♯). To flatten a note means to lower its pitch, or sound, to the next lower note on its left, ie. play the note of B followed by the black note on its immediate left. This black note is B flat (B♭).

The example below shows a black note (∗) positioned between the A and B notes. This note can be either A sharp (A♯), the A note sharpened, or B flat (B♭), the B note flattened.

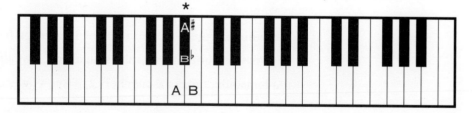

Each note on keyboard manuals and organ pedals can be raised to become a sharp (♯) or lowered to become a flat (♭). Therefore, every black note can have two names, known as enharmonic, derived from the notes on its left and right. So, a sharp sign (♯) raises a note to its right. A flat sign (♭) lowers a note to its left.

■ MUSICAL TIME

When you are reading a manuscript, various types of notes are written upon the treble and bass staves to represent a specific sound or pitch. The notes also represent musical time which is measured in beats, rather than in seconds and minutes. The form or type of the notes determines their beat value and will indicate the length of time a note is to be held when played. Rests in their various forms represent silence in music and each rest will also have a time or beat value.

Notes:	semibreve	minim	crotchet	quaver	semiquaver
	o	♩	♩	♪	♪
Beat value:	4	2	1	½	¼
Rest:	▬	▬	𝄽	𝄾	𝄿

Each note - apart from the semibreve - has a stem connected to it. In addition, the quaver has a single flag attached to the stem ♪ and the semiquaver has two flags attached to its stem ♪.

When a dot is placed by a note its beat value is increased by half as much again.

Minim + dot	♩.	2 beats + 1 beat	= total value of 3 beats
Crotchet plus dot	♩.	1 beat + ½ beat	= total value of 1 ½ beats
Quaver plus dot	♪.	½ beat + ¼ beat	= total value of ¾ beat

The dotted quaver, ¾ beat, is usually followed by the semiquaver quaver, ¼ beat, to make a total value of 1 beat of music.

Beat value ½ ¼ ¼ = 1 beat

Beat value ½ ¼ ¼ = 1 beat

For convenience, when two quavers are next to each other the flag of the first quaver will be joined to the stem of the second quaver to form a single line. The flags of the semiquavers can also be joined between notes to form a double line.

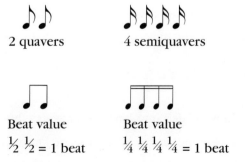

2 quavers   4 semiquavers

Beat value   Beat value
½ ½ = 1 beat   ¼ ¼ ¼ ¼ = 1 beat

I am often asked how long a beat of music lasts, or how long a minim, a crotchet or a quaver has to be held for, and many more questions on musical time. My answer is that by learning how to count evenly, in your own time, and lightly tapping on a note of the keyboard, or anything else within reach, a pattern of musical time will emerge.

Count evenly from one to four, 1-2-3-4. Repeat the counting several times and as you count tap once for each number.

1	2	3	4	1	2	3	4	1	2	3	4
tap	tap	tap	tap	tap	tap	tap	tap	tap	tap	tap	tap

Each number can represent the time value of 1 crotchet beat.

The semibreve is held and counted for four crotchet beats:

1	2	3	4	1	etc
o				o	

each note is held for four beats.

The minim is held and counted for two crotchet beats:

1	2	3	4	1	etc
♩		♩		♩	

each note is held for two beats.

The crotchet is held and counted for one beat:

1	2	3	4	1	etc
♩	♩	♩	♩	♩	

each note is held for one beat.

The quaver is held and counted for half a crotchet beat, by saying 'and' between each number - 1 and 2 and 3 and 4 and etc.: each note is held for half a beat. (When counting quavers the tap will occur on the 1 2 3 4 only and not on the 'and'.) Remember to count evenly in your own time.

The metronome, or musical clock, is the standard method of learning precise musical time and although it is now included as a feature on the rhythm unit of some electronic keyboards it is not normally used by the home musician.

Most musical arrangements include the timing sign, such as ♩ = 80 above the treble stave at the start of the music, which means that 80 crotchet beats should be played to the minute. Only the use of a metronome can ensure that the music is played exactly to the time indicated by the sign.

■ BAR LINES & TIME SIGNATURES

Each stave is divided into bars, or measures, by bar lines. In the final bar of the music two lines are drawn, these are known as double bar lines.

bar line   *bar or measure*   *double bar lines*

Each bar, or measure, divides the various types of notes and rests into groups, adding up to the 'beats in each bar', indicated by the time signature at the beginning of the music. The time signature consists of two numbers, written on the stave, one above the other, to represent the timing, or beats in the bar, of the music. The upper number is the total number of beats in each bar of the music, so if the upper number is three there are three beats in each bar and if the upper number is four there are four beats in each bar. The lower number determines which type of note receives one beat of the music. To interpret the lower number each type of note is made a division, or part of the semibreve whole note, the largest note value in modern music. When the semibreve is divided into two halves, each half represents the minim, half note. Divide the semibreve into quarters to represent the crotchet quarter note and eighths to represent the quaver eighth note etc.

semibreve	whole note	o
minim	half note	♩ ♩
crotchet	quarter note	♩ ♩ ♩ ♩
quaver	eighth note	♪ ♪ ♪ ♪ ♪ ♪ ♪ ♪
semiquaver sixteenth note		♬ ♬ ♬ ♬ ♬ ♬ ♬ ♬ ♬ ♬ ♬ ♬ ♬ ♬ ♬ ♬

A demisemiquaver is written as ♬. There are thirty two demisemiquavers in a whole note (semibreve). Space does not permit showing thirty two of them on the diagram above.

The two most common time signatures are

In the ¾ time signature the upper number is three beats to the bar and the lower number four represents the crotchet (quarter) note.

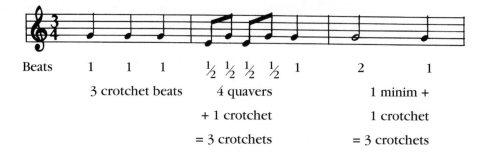

| Beats | 1 | 1 | 1 | ½ ½ ½ ½ | 1 | 2 | 1 |

3 crotchet beats   4 quavers   1 minim +

+ 1 crotchet   1 crotchet

= 3 crotchets   = 3 crotchets

Each bar can contain notes and rests of different beat values, but the total beat value of each bar will be equivalent to the time signatures.

In the $\frac{4}{4}$ time signature, the upper number is four beats in each bar and the lower number four represents the crotchet (quarter) note.

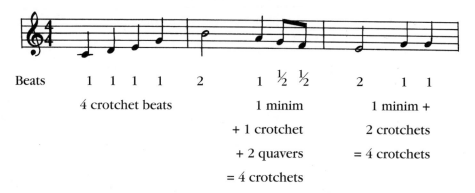

| Beats | 1 | 1 | 1 | 1 | 2 | 1 | ½ ½ | 2 | 1 | 1 |

4 crotchet beats   1 minim   1 minim +

+ 1 crotchet   2 crotchets

+ 2 quavers   = 4 crotchets

= 4 crotchets

The $\frac{4}{4}$ time signature could also be written as

known as common time.

The cut common time signature

could also be written as $\frac{2}{2}$ although this form is not normally used in popular music. The upper figure two represents two beats in each bar and the lower figure two represents the minim (half note).

$\frac{3 \text{ beats}}{4 \text{ the crotchet}}$ $\frac{4 \text{ beats}}{4 \text{ the crotchet}}$ $\frac{2 \text{ beats}}{2 \text{ the minim}}$

Cut common time usually occurs in music with a much faster tempo, when it is easier to count two minim beats than four crotchet beats in a bar.

The following illustration shows the types of notes which add up to the total beat value for each bar indicated by the ¢ time signature.

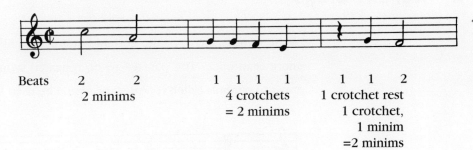

Beats   2   2   1 1 1 1   1   1   2

2 minims   4 crotchets   1 crotchet rest
= 2 minims   1 crotchet,
1 minim
=2 minims

■ TRIPLETS

A triplet is a musical term for three notes grouped together with a figure 3 written above or below them. When three quavers are grouped together in this way ♪♪♪ they are played to the time value of two quavers and are named a quaver or eighth triplet (a quaver is an eighth note of a semibreve). When three crotchets are grouped together in this way ♩♩♩ they are played to the time value of two crotchets and are named a quarter note triplet (a crotchet is a quarter note of the semibreve).

■ THE TIE

The tie is the term used for a curved line drawn above or below two or more notes, telling you to hold the first note for the total beat of the tied notes.

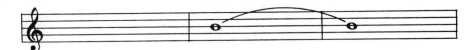

In the above illustration, the two semibreves are joined together by a tie. The first semibreve, four beats, is played and held for the total count of both notes, eight beats. Notes of different time value can be joined together by a tie but in all cases the first note is played and held for the total time value of all tied notes.

The fermata (pause) sign ⌢ tells you to hold the note over which it is written for as long as you like.

■ RHYTHM & TEMPO

Rhythm is time or movement by regular, recurring sounds, therefore musical rhythm is created by the regular pattern of beats in each bar of the music. Rhythm information can often be written as beguine, rhumba, waltz etc. at the beginning of the music.

Tempo is the speed at which you choose to play an arrangement and suggestions such as 'Moderately Slow' or 'Lively' etc. can also be written above the treble stave at the beginning of the music.

■ REPEAT SIGNS

Written music may require certain bars, or an entire passage, to be played more than once. The passage to be repeated would not be written again, musical symbols called repeat signs would be used instead.

Repeat sign B tells you to go back to repeat sign A and play the music between the signs once again. If repeat sign B only is written at the end of a number of bars, repeat from the first of the music.

Repeat symbols comprise: 'Da Capo', meaning from the beginning; 'D.C. al Fine', which means go back to the beginning and finish at the word 'Fine'; 'D.S.' (Dal Segno al Fine) repeat from the sign 𝄋 to the end. Coda is written above extra bars which have been added to a piece of music to create an ending. The Coda sign ⊕ will also appear earlier in the music to tell you when to move directly to the coda bars.

■ DOUBLE ENDINGS

Double endings consist of a number of bars at the end of a piece of music with a line over them and a number 1 in the far left corner, followed by another set of bars with a line over them and a number 2 in the left hand corner.

Play the music through with the number 1 ending to the repeat sign, then

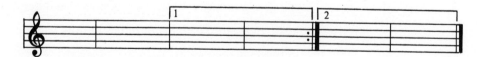

go back over the bars you have already played, play them through once again, but this time omit those bars with number 1 written above and play the number 2 ending.

■ TONES & SEMITONES

Tones and semitones are the distances between the notes on a keyboard manual. They combine in a set to form major scales, which in turn are the basis for every left hand chord.

The distance between any two notes immediately next to each other is called a semitone; these two notes can be a white note next to a black note (1), a black note next to a white note (2), or a white note next to a white note (3).

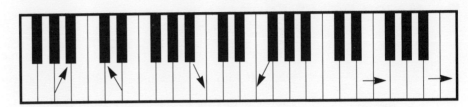

(1)
white note
to
black note

(2)
black note
to
white note

(3)
white note
to
white note

To hear a semitone distance easily, play any note on the keyboard manual, then play the note immediately next to it, up or down. Play these two notes, a semitone distance apart, one after the other - a discordant sound is produced if they are played together.

For a tone distance you must double the semitone distance so that the two semitone distances form a tone distance. Play the middle C note on the keyboard manual and then locate the note of D next to it on the right. There is a tone distance between the notes of C and D.

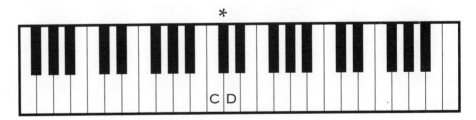

There is a black note (✳) in-between the middle C and D notes. The first semitone distance occurs between the C note and the black note (✳) and the second semitone distance occurs between the black note (✳) and the D. Therefore, C to D is a tone distance.

There is always a note in the middle of a tone distance, and there are four ways to form a tone:

(1) white note to a white note (black note in the middle);

(2) black note to a white note (white note in the middle);

(3) black note to a black note (white note in the middle);

(4) white note to a black note (white note in the middle).

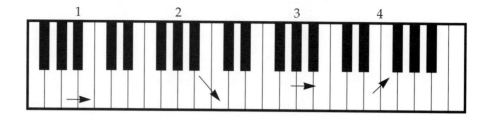

These tone distances combine with the semitone distances to form major scales, from which the left hand chords are formed.

■ MAJOR SCALE FORMATION

A major scale consists of eight notes and its name is derived from the note you start with. This first note is called the root note. To form any major scale choose a note on the keyboard manual. This now becomes the first, or root note, of the scale. Proceed to find the other seven notes using a combination of tones and semitones in the following sequence: root note, tone, tone, semitone, tone, tone, tone, semitone.

The established sequence of every major scale formation is:

starting note	root note
1. root note to 2nd note	= tone distance
2. 2nd note to 3rd note	= tone distance
3. 3rd note to 4th note	= semitone distance
4. 4th note to 5th note	= tone distance
5. 5th note to 6th note	= tone distance
6. 6th note to 7th note	= tone distance
7. 7th note to 8th note	= semitone distance
8. 8th note	= same as the root note

The notes in the above scale formation are numbered one to eight and will be used later for left hand chord construction. You do not at this stage have to practise scales, just find them.

■ THE SCALE OF C MAJOR

The C major scale is found by using the sequence established above: root note, tone, tone, semitone, tone, tone, tone, semitone. Start with the middle C.

C starting note   root note

1. C to D	= tone distance
2. D to E	= tone distance
3. E to F	= semitone distance
4. F to G	= tone distance
5. G to A	= tone distance
6. A to B	= tone distance
7. B to C	= semitone distance

8. C is the 8th note. Same name as the root note.

C	D	E	F	G	A	B	C
1	2	3	4	5	6	7	8

The C major scale is the only scale containing all white notes. As you can see, notes 1 and 8 have the same name, with each note of the scale following a consecutive alphabetical sequence. Play the C major scale on any part of the manual, between any two C notes. The 8th note of one C scale becomes the first (root note) of the next C scale.

Play the C major scale with the right hand using the fingering suggested below:

	C	D	E	F	G	A	B	C
Fingering	1	2	3	1	2	3	4	5

C	D	E	tuck thumb	F	G	A	B	C
1	2	3	under hand	1	2	3	4	5
thumb	finger	finger	to play F	thumb	finger	finger	finger	finger

■ SHARPS & FLATS IN SCALE FORMATION

Black notes are included in all major scale formations except the C major scale and as has already been established the notes of a scale follow an alphabetical sequence. To maintain the alphabetical sequence the black notes in each major scale take their name from the consecutive alphabetical letter of the scale, becoming either sharp or flat.

■ THE SCALE OF F MAJOR

The F major scale contains one black note, B♭.

Starting with the root note of F (third white note up from middle C), form the scale of F major using the established tone, semitone sequence: root note, tone, tone, semitone, tone, tone, tone, semitone.

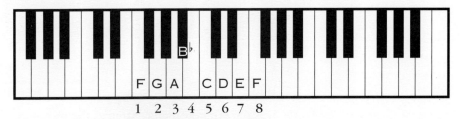

F starting note							root note
1. F to G							= tone distance
2. G to A							= tone distance
3. A to B$^\flat$							= semitone distance
4. B$^\flat$ to C							= tone distance
5. C to D							= tone distance
6. D to E							= tone distance
7. E to F							= semitone distance

8. F is the 8th note. Same name as the root note.

F	G	A	B$^\flat$	C	D	E	F
1	2	3	4	5	6	7	8

The fourth note of the F major scale is named B$^\flat$ (B flat) not A$^\sharp$, to maintain the alphabetical sequence.

Right hand fingering for the F major scale differs from that for the C major scale. The thumb is tucked under the fourth finger so that it plays the C note of the scale after the first four notes have been played.

	F	G	A	B$^\flat$	C	D	E	F
Fingering	1	2	3	4	1	2	3	4

The thumb plays F and C

■ THE SCALE OF G MAJOR

Find the G major scale using the tone, semitone sequence: root note, tone, tone, semitone, tone, tone, tone, semitone. Indeed, if you learn this sequence it will form the basis for finding every major scale and every left hand chord. So, start with the root note of G, fourth white note up from middle C.

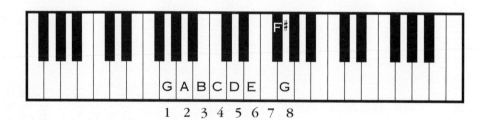

	1	2	3	4	5	6	7	8

G starting note							root note
1. G to A							= tone distance
2. A to B							= tone distance
3. B to C							= semitone distance
4. C to D							= tone distance
5. D to E							= tone distance
6. E to F$^\sharp$							= tone distance
7. F$^\sharp$ to G							= semitone distance

8. G is the 8th note. Same name as the root note.

	G	A	B	C	D	E	F#	G
Fingering	1	2	3	1	2	3	4	5

When playing the major scales allow the fingers to hover just above the manual and crawl over the notes rather than lifting the fingers high in the air between each note. This method of playing develops a smooth, flowing sequence of the eight notes of the scale and can be used effectively for playing the melody (treble stave) of music.

■ MAJOR LEFT HAND CHORD FORMATION FROM A MAJOR SCALE

A major left hand chord consists of three notes and will blend in an agreement of sound with the melody notes. When playing a left hand chord ensure that all fingers go down together, so that all the notes sound at the same time.

Chord formation is based upon specific note numbers of the major scales and once established you will be able to form every major chord.

Every major chord - in its root position - is formed from the first (root note), third note and fifth note of the major scale.

Formation of the C major chord

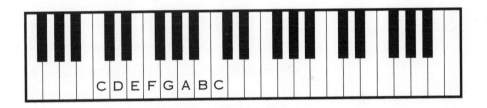

1 2 3 4 5 6 7 8	note nos. of C major scale
1 3 5	note nos. of C major chord
C - E - G	C major chord

Formation of the F major chord

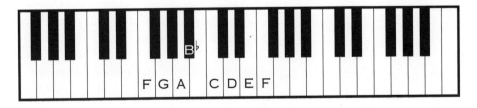

1 2 3 4 5 6 7 8	note nos. of F major scale
1 3 5	note nos. of F major chord
F - A - C	F major chord

Formation of the G major chord

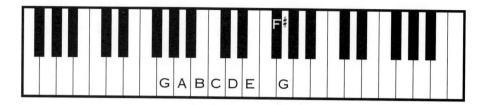

1	2	3	4	5	6	7	8	note nos. of G major scale
1		3		5				note nos. of G major chord
G	-	B	-	D				G major chord

INVERSIONS OF A MAJOR CHORD

An inversion of a chord is a change in position of one of the notes, while the other notes of the chord remain unchanged. Every major chord has two inversions. The first inversion of a major chord uses the same notes as the major chord, however, the first, or root note, moves its position from the extreme left to the extreme right of the chord, while the third and fifth notes remain in the same position. In the second inversion of a major chord the third note moves its position from the extreme left to the extreme right of the chord, while the fifth and eighth notes stay in the same position.

The note numbers of the major chord are 1 - 3 - 5; the note numbers of the first inversion are 3 - 5 - - 8(1); the note numbers of the second inversion are 5 - - 8(1) - 3. The dashes which separate the note numbers of the major chords represent the unplayed notes of the major scale.

C major chord & inversions

C major chord	1st inversion	2nd inversion
1 3 5	3 5 8(1)	5 8(1) 3
C - E - G	E - G - - C	G - - C - E

F major chord & inversions

F major chord	1st inversion	2nd inversion
1 3 5	3 5 8(1)	5 8(1) 3
F - A - C	A - C - - F	C - - F - A

G major chord & inversions

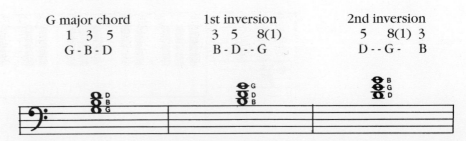

LEFT HAND CHORD POSITIONS ON THE LOWER ORGAN MANUAL

On a dual manual organ left hand chords will be played within the two notes F to F either side of middle C on the lower manual. By containing them in this small area, chord changing will be smoother as each chord will be positioned close to the next chord in the music. Every chord, with the exception of thirteenths, can be played within this section of the manual.

Lower manual

Chord playing position

Bass stave

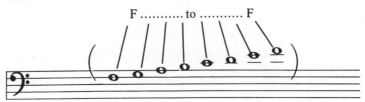

Keep the wrists still when playing chords and create finger movement only within this small area of the keyboard manual to enable you to change chords easily. Dual manual organ players can ignore the rest of the lower manual at this stage.

The second inversion of the C major chord, G - - C - E, is played between the two notes of F either side of middle C.

C chord position between the notes F & F

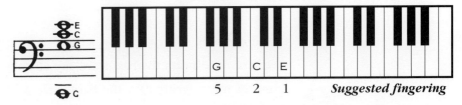

Suggested fingering

Initially the root note of C in the C major chord is played on the dual manual organ as the pedal note with each C major chord and its inversions.

F chord position between the notes of F & F

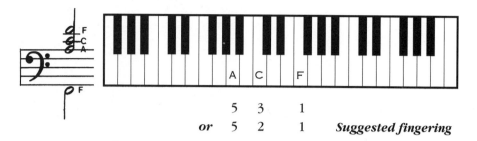

5   3   1
or   5   2   1   *Suggested fingering*

The F major chord and its first inversion both have their notes between F and F. The first inversion is illustrated above. This is usually played for ease of chord changing.

The F bass pedal is played with the F major chord or its inversions.

G chord position between the notes of F & F

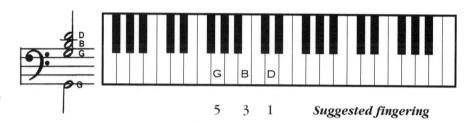

5   3   1   *Suggested fingering*

The root position of the G major chord is played between the two F notes and the G pedal is played with the G major chord or inversions.

■ THE TRADITIONAL BASS STAVE

There are two ways of reading music for playing left hand chords and bass pedal notes. The traditional method involves reading the bass stave upon which groups of notes are written to represent the chords. A single note

shows the accompanying bass pedal, although the pedal note can sometimes occupy a bass stave of its own.

■ READING CHORD SYMBOLS

Chord symbols, which can be written above the treble stave, between staves, or underneath the bass stave, are an abbreviation of the name of the group of notes written on the bass stave as the left hand chord and its accompanying bass pedal note.

Each chord symbol consists of an alphabetical letter which can be followed by a number, such as 7, 6 etc., or a small (m). Each alphabetical letter represents a major left hand chord and any instructions following the letter (7, 6, m etc.) are telling you to adapt the major chord. The chord symbols for the major chords are: C for C major, F for F major and G for G major.

Chord symbols written above the treble stave

Chord symbols

Each chord symbol also tells you which note to play as the pedal note with each left hand chord, ie. play the C pedal note with each chord of C, the F pedal note with each chord of F, etc.

Many books of music are written with a single treble stave and chord symbols (shown below).

Chord symbols

The advantages of reading this form of music include instant sight reading, as there is less information to take in at once and the music is condensed to avoid unnecessary page turning. The chord symbols, when used to their fullest extent, can convey to advanced players not only a left hand chord and bass pedal note, but also chord progressions, counter melody, right hand chords and harmony movements. These advanced subjects are included in Parts II and III of this book.

■ MAJOR LEFT HAND CHORD STRUCTURE

We have now established the rule for finding any major chord with the notes 1 - 3 - 5 from any major scale. Once this chord has been formed, it can be built upon, or adapted to form other chords of the same name.

If you refer to the following chord structure you will see how the major chord forms the basis of sixth, seventh and major seventh chords and also minor, minor sixth and minor seventh chords. The 'main feature' column tells you which notes of the major chord can be adapted and which notes of the scale (from which the major chord was formed) are added to the major chord.

To form a sixth chord, simply add the sixth note of the scale to the first, third and fifth notes of the major chord, giving a four note chord of 1 - 3 - 5 6.

A seventh chord is formed upon the major chord of 1 - 3 - 5 by adding the seventh note of scale flattened by a semitone: $1 - 3 - 5 - 7^\flat$. Written as $7^\flat$ to distinguish it from the normal seventh note of the scale, the $7^\flat$ note is a whole tone below note number eight.

Each major sixth and seventh chord becomes a minor chord by flattening the third note (of scale) within the chord by a semitone.

The major seventh chord also contains four notes and is formed by adding the seventh note of scale to the major chord: 1 - 3 - 5 - 7. The seventh note of scale is only a semitone below note number eight.

Chord structure of major to major 7th chords

Chord name	main feature	note numbers of major scale	chord symbol
major	notes of major scale	1-3-5	G
major 6th	added 6th of scale	1-3-5 6	G6
7th	added $7^\flat$ of scale	$1\text{-}3\text{-}5\text{-}7^\flat$	G7
minor	flat 3rd of major chord	$1\text{-}3^\flat 5$	Gm
minor 6th	flat 3rd, added 6th	$1\text{-}3^\flat\text{-}5\ 6$	Gm6
minor 7th	flat 3rd, added $7^\flat$	$1\text{-}3^\flat\text{-}5\text{-}7^\flat$	Gm7
major 7th	added 7th of scale	1-3-5-7	Gmaj7

When you have studied the G chord structure below, find the G major chord (G - B - D) and hold on to it. Add the sixth note of the G major scale to play the G6 chord, G - B - D E. Substitute the note of F natural ($7^\flat$) for the note of E to play the G7 chord, G - B - D - F♯. Turn the G, G6 and G7 chords into minor chords by flattening the third note of B to B♭ in each chord. To play the G major seventh chord simply add the normal seventh note of F♯. From the G major scale, to the G major chord.

Basic chord structure of G chords from the G major scale shown in relation to the lower organ manual

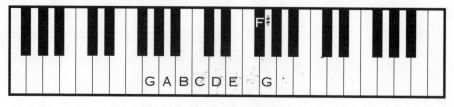

major	G - B - D	1 - 3 - 5
major 6th	G - B - D E	1 - 3 - 5 6
7th	G - B - D - F♮	1 - 3 - 5 - 7♭
minor	G - B♭ - D	1 - 3♭ - 5
minor 6th	G - B♭ - D E	1 - 3♭ - 5 6
minor 7th	G - B♭ - D - F♮	1 - 3♭ - 5 - 7♭
major 7th	G - B - D - F♯	1 - 3 - 5 - 7

The chords of G can be played in their formation position between F and F on the lower manual accompanied by the G pedal note to name each G chord.

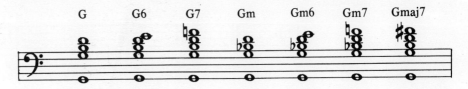

Basic chord structure of F chords from the F major scale shown in relation to the lower organ manual

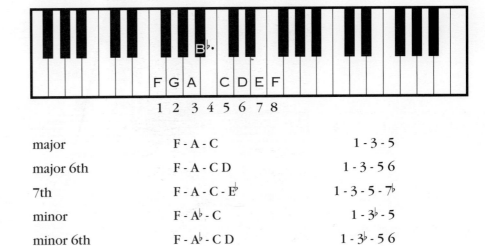

major	F - A - C	1 - 3 - 5
major 6th	F - A - C D	1 - 3 - 5 6
7th	F - A - C - E♭	1 - 3 - 5 - 7♭
minor	F - A♭ - C	1 - 3♭ - 5
minor 6th	F - A♭ - C D	1 - 3♭ - 5 6
minor 7th	F - A♭ - C - E♭	1 - 3♭ - 5 - 7♭
major 7th	F - A - C - E	1 - 3 - 5 - 7

The chords of F in their formation position (or their first inversion) will be in the correct playing position and will be accompanied by the F pedal note.

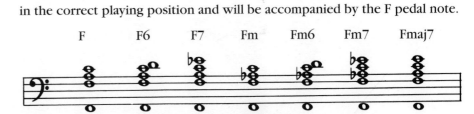

Basic chord structure of C chords from the C major scale shown in relation to the lower organ manual

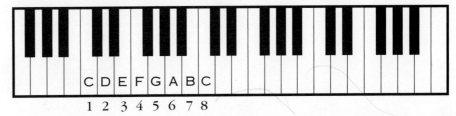

major	C - E - G	1 - 3 - 5
major 6th	C - E - G A	1 - 3 - 5 6
7th	C - E - G - B$^\flat$	1 - 3 - 5 - 7$^\flat$
minor	C - E$^\flat$ - G	1 - 3$^\flat$ - 5
minor 6th	C - E$^\flat$ - G A	1 - 3$^\flat$ - 5 6
minor 7th	C - E$^\flat$ - G - B$^\flat$	1 - 3$^\flat$ - 5 - 7$^\flat$
major 7th	C - E - G - B	1 - 3 - 5 - 7

Root position

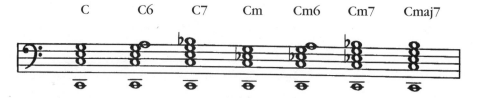

All chords of C will need to be inverted to be played in the correct position between the notes of F to F on the lower organ manual and accompanied by the C pedal.

Playing position

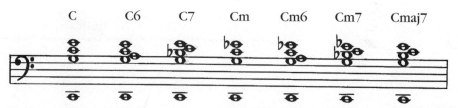

Below is given a complete table of major scales for forming your own chord structures.

■ MAJOR SCALES

	1	2	3	4	5	6	7	8
F$^\sharp$	F$^\sharp$	G$^\sharp$	A$^\sharp$	B	C$^\sharp$	D$^\sharp$	- E$^\sharp$	F$^\sharp$
B	B	C$^\sharp$	D$^\sharp$	E	F$^\sharp$	G$^\sharp$	A$^\sharp$	B
E	E	F$^\sharp$	G$^\sharp$	A	B	C$^\sharp$	D$^\sharp$	E
A	A	B	C$^\sharp$	D	E	F$^\sharp$	G$^\sharp$	A
D	D	E	F$^\sharp$	G	A	B	C$^\sharp$	D
G	G	A	B	C	D	E	F$^\sharp$	G
C	C	D	E	F	G	A	B	C
F	F	G	A	B$^\flat$	C	D	E	F
B$^\flat$	B$^\flat$	C	D	E$^\flat$	F	G	A	B$^\flat$
E$^\flat$	E$^\flat$	F	G	A$^\flat$	B$^\flat$	C	D	E$^\flat$
A$^\flat$	A$^\flat$	B$^\flat$	C	D$^\flat$	E$^\flat$	F	G	A$^\flat$
D$^\flat$	D$^\flat$	E$^\flat$	F	G$^\flat$	A$^\flat$	B$^\flat$	C	D$^\flat$
G$^\flat$	G$^\flat$	A$^\flat$	B$^\flat$	C$^\flat$	D$^\flat$	E$^\flat$	F	G$^\flat$

Further on in this book I will show you how to extend the chord structure to form the remaining chords from major seventh to thirteenths from a major scale. You can also participate to find the E♭ chords from the E♭ major scale and can complete your knowledge of chord formations by learning how to play diminished seventh and augmented chords as well as chords with a suspended fourth note. You should never again feel unable to play an arrangement with unfamiliar chords.

■ KEY SIGNATURES

Now that you understand major scale formation, you can learn how to recognise a key signature.

A key signature consists of sharps (♯) or flats (♭) written on the stave after the treble and bass clef signs, but before the time signature. A composer or arranger will establish a key in which the music is to be written. The sharps or flats, from the scale of the same name as the key, are then written upon the stave as the key signature of the music to illustrate which key you are playing in.

A key signature performs two functions. Firstly, the sharps or flats of the key signature tell you which notes in the music are to be sharpened or flattened and secondly, as will be explained in the next part of the book, the key signature helps you identify which left hand chords will occur in each key of music. Therefore, before starting to play you must read the key signature to identify the major scale from which the sharps or flats are taken. The name of the scale will also be the name of the key you are playing in.

In example 1, below, one sharpened note, F♯, from the scale of G major, is written on the staves to tell you that the music is in the key of G major. All notes of F in the music will be played as F♯ in this key.

Example 1

Scale of G major
G   A   B   C   D   E   F♯   G

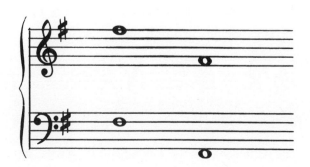

In example 2, below, one flattened note, B♭, from the scale of F major is written on the staves to tell you that you are playing in the key of F major. All notes of B in the music will be played as B♭ when playing in this key.

Example 2

Scale of F major

F   G   A   B♭   C   D   E   F

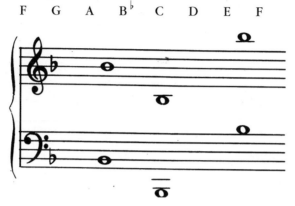

■ ACCIDENTALS

A sharp or a flat sign preceding a note in the music is called an accidental and it will sharpen or flatten the note it is written against. The accidental normally applies only for the duration of the bar in which it occurs.

Bar 1   Bar 2   Bar3

In the above illustration the only notes to be sharpened normally would be the notes of F as directed by the F♯ note in the key signature, but the accidental sign (♯) preceding the first note of C in the second bar indicates that that note is to be played as C♯ for the duration of the bar. The note of F (∗) in the third and fourth bars must be played as F♯, as in the key signature.

■ NATURAL SIGNS

A natural sign (♮) is written before a note to cancel a sharp or flat note in the key signature or a previous accidental.

The natural sign in the second and third bars of the illustration cancels the B♭ note indicated by the B♭ key signature so the notes are played as B natural.

■ OCTAVES

An octave consists of eight notes and is the distance between any two notes of the same name; C to C, G to G, A to A etc. A scale is an octave as it has eight notes, beginning and ending on the same note.

The '8va' sign above the treble stave tells you to play the notes on the manuscript an octave higher than written and the duration of this sign is the length of the dotted line over the notes to be played in this way.

■ CHORD CHANGING

Smooth chord changing is achieved by the correct playing position and by holding on to a common note between chords if possible.

For example, when changing between a C and G7 chord, hold on to the G note which occurs in both chords:

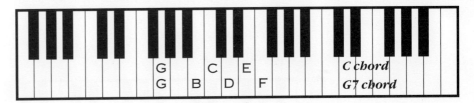

Play the C chord	G	C	E
Pivot note held	G		
Finger movement		B	F♯
Added note of G7 chord:		D	
G7 chord	G	B	D	F♯
back to C chord	G	C	E

Change the pedal note on the organ from C to G as the chords are changed. When changing between a C and F chord hold on to the note of C in both chords.

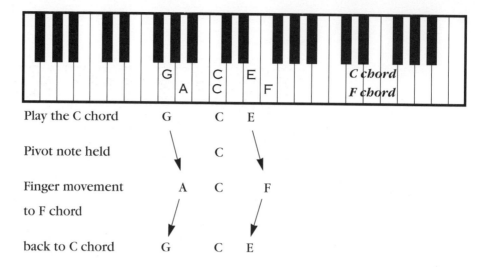

Play the C chord	G		C	E	
Pivot note held			C		
Finger movement to F chord		A	C		F
back to C chord	G		C	E	

Change the pedal note on the organ from C to F as the chords are changed. The left hand should move as little as possible to give fluency to playing left hand chords.

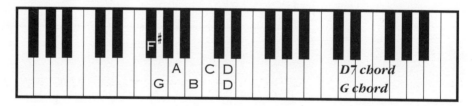

When changing between a G and D7 chord hold on to the common note of D in both chords.

Play the G major chord	G	B	D
Pivot note held			D
Finger movement	F#	A	D
Added note of D7 chord			C
D7 chord	F#	A	C D
followed by G major	G	B	D

The pedal is changed from G to D as the chords are changed.

When changing between the E♭ and Cm chords hold on to the common note of G and E♭.

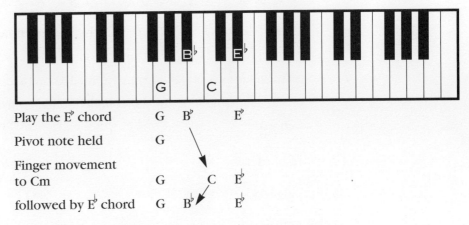

Play the E♭ chord   G   B♭   E♭

Pivot note held   G

Finger movement
to Cm   G   C   E♭

followed by E♭ chord   G   B♭   E♭

The pedal changes from E♭ to C as the chords are changed.

The following pages show you how to form the more advanced chords to thirteenths. Try to become as familiar with playing them as you are with the basic chords of C, F and G etc. These chords are not physically more difficult to play, so include them in your music instead of ignoring them, as far too many players seem to do.

■ EXTENDING THE CHORD STRUCTURE FOR ADVANCED CHORDS

The chord structure can now be extended to include advanced chords of ninth, eleventh and various forms of thirteenth, but before forming these chords an extended scale sequence must be established.

Each note of a major scale is numbered one to eight, therefore note number eight of the scale is also note number one of the next scale sequence.

G major scale sequence 1   2 3 4 5 6   78(1)2 3 4   5 6 etc.

9 1011 1213 advanced
chord note
numbers

In any major scale sequence, the eighth note is also the first note, the second note is also the ninth note, the third note is also the tenth note, and so on.

A thirteenth chord will contain the highest note number (13) of a major scale sequence to be used for chord formation.

The major to major seventh chord structure has been set out in the following table to show the complete build-up from a major to a thirteenth chord.

Chord name	Note nos. of major scale
major	1 - 3 - 5
6th	1 - 3 - 5 6
7th	1 - 3 - 5 - 7$^\flat$
minor	1 - 3$^\flat$ - 5
minor 6th	1 - 3$^\flat$ - 5 6
minor 7th	1 - 3$^\flat$ - 5 - 7$^\flat$
major 7th	1 - 3 - 5 - 7
major 9th	1 - 3 - 5 - 7 - 9
9th	1 - 3 - 5 - 7$^\flat$ - 9
11th	1 - - - 5 - 7$^\flat$ - 9 - 11
13th	1 - - - - - 7$^\flat$ 8 - 10 - - 13
13th (9)	1 - - - - - 7$^\flat$ - 9 10 - - 13
13th (9 & 11)	1 - - - - - 7$^\flat$ - 9 - 11 - 13

Advanced chord formations do not include the root note as part of the chord. The root note is played as the pedal note naming the chord. Using the G major scale and chords as an example, the G major ninth chord starts its formation upon the third note of B from the G major scale. The root note of G is played as the pedal note and the other four notes of B - D - F$^\sharp$ - A (3 - 5 - 7 - 9) as the left hand chord.

The G ninth, eleventh and thirteenth chords include the 7$^\flat$ note (F$^\natural$) of the G major scale in their formation although the starting note for chord formation will vary. The root pedal note of G is played with each G chord. For instance, the ninth chord starts its formation upon the third note of B, the eleventh chord starts its formation upon the fifth note of D and the thirteenth chord starts upon the 7$^\flat$ note of F$^\natural$.

	1	2	3	4	5	6	7	8	9	10	11	12	13	
G major	G	-	B	-	D									G
G 6th	G	-	B	-	D	E								G6
G 7th	G	-	B	-	D	-	F♮							G7
G minor	G	-	B♭	-	D									Gm
G minor 6th	G	-	B♭	-	D	E								Gm6
G minor 7th	G	-	B♭	-	D	-	F♮							Gm7
G major 7th	G	-	B	-	D	-	F#							Gmaj7
G major 9th	G	-	B	-	D	-	F#	-	A					Gmaj9
G 9th	G	-	B	-	D	-	F♮	-	A					G9
G 11th	G	-	-	-	D	-	F♮	-	A	-	C			G11
G 13	G	-	-	-	-	-	F♮	G	-	B	-	-	E	G13
G 13 (9)	G	-	-	-	-	-	F♮	-	A	B	-	-	E	G13(9)
G 13 (9 & 11)	G	-	-	-	-	-	F♮	-	A	-	C	-	E	G13(9&11)

The chords of G major ninth, G ninth and G eleventh will need to be inverted to be played between F and F as shown on the bass stave below.

Gmaj9   G 9   G11   G13   G13(9)   G13(9&11)

The G13 chords should be played an octave lower on the manual than their formation position, as shown on the bass stave above.

Below is illustrated the extended chord structure from the F major scale, starting with the F major seventh chord. The root note of F is played as the pedal note with each F chord.

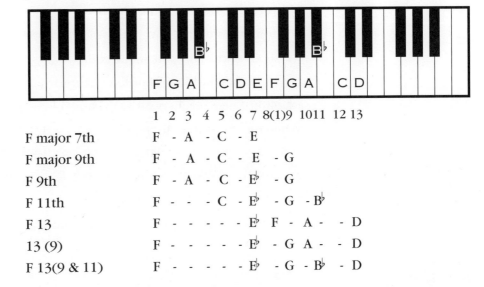

	1	2	3	4	5	6	7	8(1)	9	10	11	12	13
F major 7th	F	-	A	-	C	-	E						
F major 9th	F	-	A	-	C	-	E	-	G				
F 9th	F	-	A	-	C	-	E♭	-	G				
F 11th	F	-	-	-	C	-	E♭	-	G	-	B♭		
F 13	F	-	-	-	-	-	E♭	F	-	A	-	-	D
13 (9)	F	-	-	-	-	-	E♭	-	G	A	-	-	D
F 13(9 & 11)	F	-	-	-	-	-	E♭	-	G	-	B♭	-	D

Next is illustrated the extended chord structure from the C major scale, starting with the C major 7th chord. The root note of C is played as the pedal note with each C chord.

	1	2	3	4	5	6	7	8(1)	9	10	11	12	13
C major 7th	C	-	E	-	G	-	B						
C major 9th	C	-	E	-	G	-	B	-	D				
C 9th	C	-	E	-	G	-	B♭	-	D				
C 11th	C	-	-	-	G	-	B♭	-	D	-	F		
C 13	C	-	-	-	-	-	B♭	C	-	E	-	-	A
C 13 (9)	C	-	-	-	-	-	B♭	-	D	E	-	-	A
C 13 (9 & 11)	C	-	-	-	-	-	B♭	-	D	-	F	-	A

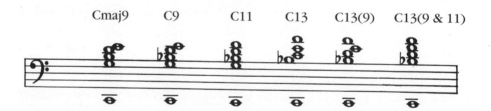

Thirteenth chords will not be inverted but played in their formation position, or an octave lower, to avoid the semitone discord between the $7^♭$ and sixth (thirteenth) note in the chord.

Try to build your own chord structure from the major scales using the established note numbers for each chord or complete the following exercise to find the E♭ chords from the E♭ major scale.

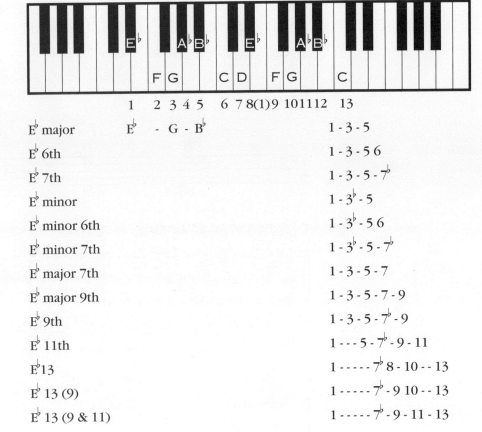

	1	2 3 4 5	6 7 8(1)9 10 11 12	13

E♭ major	E♭ - G - B♭	1 - 3 - 5
E♭ 6th		1 - 3 - 5 6
E♭ 7th		1 - 3 - 5 - 7♭
E♭ minor		1 - 3♭ - 5
E♭ minor 6th		1 - 3♭ - 5 6
E♭ minor 7th		1 - 3♭ - 5 - 7♭
E♭ major 7th		1 - 3 - 5 - 7
E♭ major 9th		1 - 3 - 5 - 7 - 9
E♭ 9th		1 - 3 - 5 - 7♭ - 9
E♭ 11th		1 - - - 5 - 7♭ - 9 - 11
E♭13		1 - - - - - 7♭ 8 - 10 - - 13
E♭ 13 (9)		1 - - - - - 7♭ - 9 10 - - 13
E♭ 13 (9 & 11)		1 - - - - - 7♭ - 9 - 11 - 13

The first inversion of the E♭ chords will all be in the correct playing position between F and F, except for the E♭13 chords which are played an octave lower. Play the root note of E♭ as the pedal note with each chord. The complete E♭ chord structure is given further on in this section.

Other chords can be written in the music, such as diminished sevenths, augmented fifths, augmented sevenths and chords with a suspended note.

Diminished seventh chords are formed from the major chord by flattening the third and fifth notes by a semitone and adding the seventh note of scale flattened twice:

diminished 7th chord	1 - 3♭ - 5♭ - 7♭♭	flat 3rd & 5th '7♭♭'

Using the C major chord as an example, C - E - G, the root note of C is unaltered, the third note of E is flattened to E♭ and the fifth note of G is flattened to G♭. The seventh note of the C major scale (B) is then flattened twice, first to B♭ and then to A and added to the chord.

The notes of the C diminished seventh chord are C - E♭ - G♭ A.

Use the same method to form the F diminished seventh chord from the F major chord, F - A - C: flatten the third and fifth notes to A♭ and C♭ (B) before adding the seventh note of the F major scale, E, flattened twice to D.

The notes of the F diminished seventh chord are F - A♭ - B - D.

To form the G diminished seventh chord from the G major chord, G - B - D, flatten the third and fifth notes to B♭ and D♭ before adding the seventh note of the G major scale, F♯, flattened twice to E. The notes of the G diminished seventh chord are G - B♭ - D♭ - E.

The diminished seventh chord symbols can be written as C°7 or Cdim7.

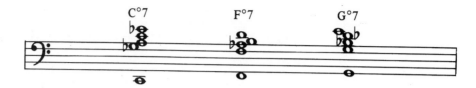

Create inversions of the diminished seventh chords to play them between F and F. By holding each chord and playing each of the four notes as the pedal note, you are actually playing four different diminished seventh chords without moving your left hand at all.

The four diminished seventh chords of G°7, B♭°7, D♭°7 and E°7, are named on the organ by changing the pedal note while the G°7 chord is held:

G diminished 7	(G B♭ D♭ E)	played with a G pedal
B♭ diminished 7	(G B♭ D♭ E)	played with a B♭ pedal
D♭ diminished 7	(G B♭ D♭ E)	played with a D♭ pedal
E diminished 7	(G B♭ D♭ E)	played with an E pedal

Two other sets of four diminished seventh chords can be created from the C diminished seventh and F diminished seventh chords. Just hold each diminished seventh chord and play each of the four notes in the chord as the pedal note to name all other diminished seventh chords in each set.

■ AUGMENTED FIFTH CHORDS

An augmented fifth chord is formed from the notes of the major chord by sharpening the fifth note of the chord by a semitone.

Augmented fifth chord	1 - 3 - 5♯
C augmented fifth	C - E - G♯

The chord symbol for the augmented fifth chord can be either Caug or C+.

The augmented seventh chord is a normal seventh chord with its fifth note sharpened by a semitone.

Augmented seventh chord	1 - 3 - 5♯ - ♭7
C augmented seventh	C - E - G♯ - B♭

The chord symbol for this chord can be either Caug7 or C7+.

A major chord containing a suspended note is formed from the first, fourth and fifth notes of the major scale. When these three notes have been played as a chord, the fourth note will usually 'resolve' or pass to the third note while the first and fifth notes are held, to play a major chord.

Major chord with	1 - - 4 5	notes of the major scale
suspended note:	1 - 3 - 5	4th note resolving to 3rd note
	1 - 3 - 5	notes of the major scale

C with suspended	1 - - 4 5	
4th note	C - - F G	Chord symbol Csus
C major chord	C - E♭ - G	or Csus4
	1 - 3 - 5	

A seventh chord with a suspended note is formed from the first, fourth, fifth and 7♭ notes of the major scale. The fourth note will usually 'resolve' or pass to the third note to play the normal seventh chord.

7th chord with suspended 4th note:

	1 - - 4 5 - 7♭	notes of major scale
C 7th suspended	C - - F G - B♭	4th note
normal 7th chord	C - E♭ G - B♭	resolving to 3rd note

Chord symbol C7sus or C7sus4.

A chord containing a suspended note may sound 'off-key' when first played but this effect will disappear when the fourth note moves to the third note of the normal major or seventh chords.

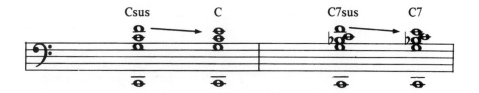

■ CHORDS THAT LOOK FAMILIAR

When forming a left hand chord you may realise that you have played exactly the same notes before as a chord with another name. If you play a C6 chord (G A - C - E) with a C pedal note and hold these notes while you change the pedal note to A, you are playing an Am7 chord, G A - C - E. The notes F - A - C D, played with an F pedal note, form an F6 chord, but if you change the pedal note to D with the same notes (F - A - C D), you are playing a Dm7 chord.

Each major seventh chord will have the same notes as a minor chord, when its root note is omitted to avoid the semitone discord between the seventh and eighth (1) notes.

Notes of a Cmaj7 chord	G - B - - E	C pedal, 2nd inversion root omitted,
are the notes of an Em chord	G♯ - B - - E	when played with an E pedal
Notes of an A♭maj7 chord	G - - C - E♭	A♭ pedal, 3rd inversion, root omitted
are the notes of a Cm chord	G - - C - E♭	when played with C pedal
Notes of a D♭maj7 chord	A♭ - C - - F	D♭ pedal, 2nd inversion, root omitted
are the notes of an Fm chord	A♭ - C - - F	when played with F pedal

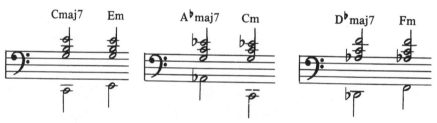

Each ninth chord will have the same notes as a minor sixth chord.

Notes of a C9 chord	G - B♭ - D E	C pedal, 1st inversion,
are the notes of a Gm6 chord	G - B♭ - D E	when played with G pedal
Notes of a B9 chord	F♯ - A - C♯ - D♯	B pedal, 2nd inversion,
are the notes of an F♯m6 chord	F♯ - A♮ - C♯ D♯	when played with an F♯ pedal

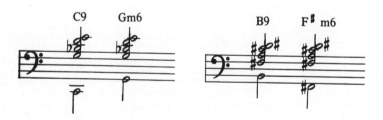

The chords shown above are all in their correct inversions between F and F.

Each minor seventh chord will have the same notes as a sixth chord.

The Bm7 and D6 chords have the same notes:

$$F♯ - A \; B - D \quad \text{(B or D pedal).}$$

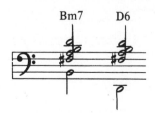

The Em7 and G6 chords have the same notes:

G - B - D E   (E or G pedal)

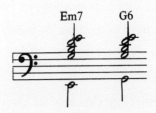

The Am7 and C6 chords have the same notes:

G A - C - E   (A or C pedal).

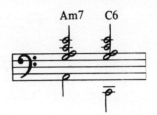

The Dm7 and F6 chords have the same notes:

F - A - C D   (D or F pedal)

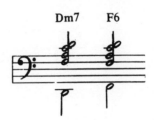

Each seventh chord with an added flat 9, such as C7($^\flat$9) will have the same notes as a diminished chord:

The notes of a C7($^\flat$9) chord,	G B$^\flat$*D$^\flat$ E	(with a C pedal),
are the notes of a Gdim7 chord,	G B$^\flat$ D$^\flat$ E	(with a G pedal),
as well as being the notes of an A7($^\flat$9) chord.	G B$^\flat$*D$^\flat$ E	(with an A pedal).
The notes of a D7($^\flat$9) chord,	F$^\sharp$ A C *E$^\flat$	(with a D pedal),
are the notes of a F$^\sharp$dim7 chord,	F$^\sharp$ A C *D$^\sharp$	(with an F$^\sharp$ pedal),
as well as being the notes of a B7($^\flat$9) chord,	F$^\sharp$ A C *D$^\sharp$	(with a B pedal).

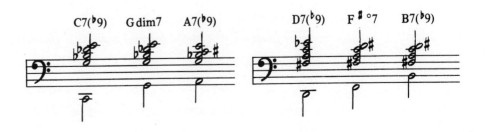

In the first example of the C7($\flat$9) and A7($\flat$9) the *D$\flat$ and *C$\sharp$ notes are an enharmonic change, which means that although the name of the note changes, its position or pitch remains unchanged. The C$\sharp$note in the A7($\flat$9) chord is the note of the A major scale. It could not be named D$\flat$. The same applies to the *E$\flat$ note in the D7($\flat$9) chord and the *D$\sharp$ note in the B7($\flat$9) chord.

Another example of chord similarity is between m7($\flat$5) chords and m6 chords:

the F$\sharp$m7($\flat$5) has the same notes as an Am6,

F$\sharp$ - A - C - E   (F$\sharp$ or A pedal);

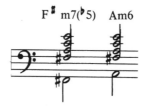

the Bm7($\flat$5) has the same notes as a Dm6,

F$\sharp$ - A B - D   (B or D pedal);

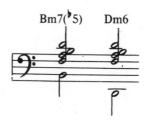

the Em7($\flat$5) has the same notes as a Gm6,

G - B$\flat$ - D E   (E or G pedal).

The problem of remembering the formation of advanced chords can be helped by visualising the easier, more familiar chords with the same note formation. Ensure that the root note played on the pedal names the chord written in the music, do not play the root note of the easier chord being visualised.

For example, the chord symbol is A$\flat$maj7, visualise a Cm chord:

visualise   Cm G - - C E$\flat$ (normally C pedal)

play A$\flat$ maj7   G - - C E$\flat$ with an A$\flat$ pedal

(the root note is omitted in the inversion of the A$\flat$maj7 chord),

If the chord symbol is F$\sharp$m7($\flat$5), visualise an Am6 chord:

visualise Am6 F$^\sharp$ - A - C$^\natural$ - E (normally A pedal)

play F$^\sharp$ m7($\flat$5) F$^\sharp$ - A$^\natural$ - C$^\natural$ - E with an F$^\sharp$ pedal.

■ INTERPRETATION OF SIGNS ADDED TO CHORD SYMBOLS

Left hand chords can be altered in various ways. These chord alterations and additions are written in brackets, after the chord name and will include sharpened and flattened notes of the major scale from which the chord was formed.

Using the C major scale as an example, some of the additional chord signs are shown below:

C major scale

	C D E F G A B C D	
	1 2 3 4 5 6 7 8 9	
C($^\sharp$5) or (+5)	C - E - G$^\sharp$	5th note sharpened
C($^\flat$5) or (-5)	C - E - G$^\flat$	5th note flattened
C($^\sharp$7) or (+7)	C - E - G - B	7th note added to chord
C($^\sharp$9) Pedal	C G - - C D$^\sharp$	9th note sharpened
C7($^\flat$9) or (-9)		
Pedal	C - E - G - B$^\flat$ - D$^\flat$	9th note flattened
C7(9) or (C9)		
Pedal	C - E - G - B$^\flat$ - D	9th note added to 7th chord

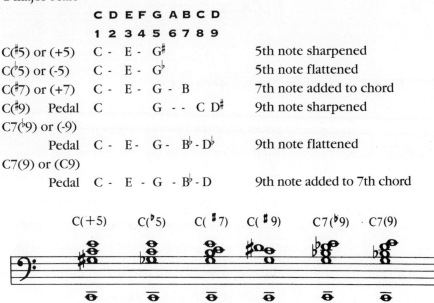

The following chord structure highlights the main feature that alters each chord.

Chord symbol	note numbers of any major scale	main feature
Cm7($^\flat$5)	1 - 3$^\flat$ - 5$^\flat$ - 7$^\flat$	flat 5th note
C(+7) C($^\sharp$7)	1 - 3 - 5 - 7	7th included
C7($^\sharp$9)	1 - 3 - 5 - 7$^\flat$ - 9$^\sharp$ pedal —— chord ——	9th sharpened
C7($^\flat$9) C7(-9)	1 - 3 - 5 - 7$^\flat$ - 9$^\flat$ pedal —— chord ——	9th flattened
		added notes
C(6/9)	1 - - - 5 6 - 8 9 pedal —chord —	added 9th (3 & 7$^\flat$ omitted)
C7(11)	1 - - - 5 - 7$^\flat$ 8 - - 11 pedal —— chord ——	added 11th (3 & 9 omitted)
Cm7(11)	1 - (3$^\flat$) - - 7$^\flat$ 8 - 10$^\flat$11 pedal ——chord ——	added 11th (5 omitted) (3$^\flat$) becomes 10$^\flat$

■ PICK-UP NOTES

Pick-up notes lead into the first bar of the music and do not usually add up to the total beat value of one bar indicated by the time signature. Add the value of the pick-up notes to the notes in the last bar to equal the total beat value of one bar of the music.

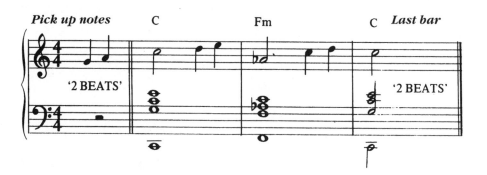

■ PLAYING THE BASS PEDALS

Shoes need not be removed to play the bass pedals, although a light shoe or slipper can help to get the feel of the notes and also achieve the smooth movement of coaxing the pedals down rather than hitting them sharply. The left foot should hover above the pedal board ready to create a similar technique to crawling over the melody notes on the manual.

Up to now, the single pedal note played with the left hand chord has been the root note of each chord and also the root note of the scale from which the left hand chord was formed.

Initially, one pedal note in each bar is sufficient, whether playing in ¾ or ⁴⁄₄ time, but when playing to rhythm the single pedal note may seem inadequate and the left foot will want to move in time. You can sustain left hand chords while a second pedal note is added to each bar when playing in ⁴⁄₄ time. The root note of each chord will be played on the first beat and repeated on the third beat in each bar for a double pedal rhythmic effect.

Double pedal notes in each bar

When you are proficient in playing the double pedal rhythm, try the alternating pedal movement to play a root and fifth pedal rhythm.

The two notes of a root and fifth pedal rhythm are the root note which you have already been playing and also the fifth note duplicated from the left hand chord or scale from which the left hand chord was formed.

For music written with a $\frac{4}{4}$ time signature, the root and fifth pedal notes will be played on the first and third beats in each bar and each pedal note has the time value of a minim. The left hand chords can be sustained for the four beats in each bar.

In the first illustration (fig. 1), the music is written in the key of G major with an F♯ key signature. The G major chord in the first two bars is accompanied by the root pedal note of G followed by the fifth note of D in each bar. The two notes of G and D are the root and fifth notes of the G major chord and also the root and fifth notes of the G major scale. When the left hand chord changes to D7 for the third and fourth bars of the illustration, the root note of D followed by the fifth note of A from the D7 chord (or D major scale) are played as the pedal notes.

Fig 1 Illustrations of traditional bass stave & chord symbols to play root & fifth pedal rhythm

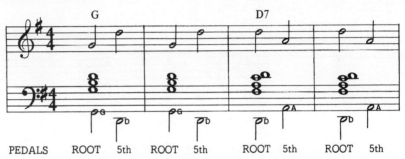

From the first basic movement in fig. 1 create a rhythmic left hand chord accompaniment to a variation of the root and fifth pedal technique, known as pedal - chord - pedal - chord movement.

In fig. 2 the music is again written in the key of G major with a $\frac{4}{4}$ time signature and identical chords and pedal notes as in fig. 1. The root and fifth pedal notes, played on the first and third beats in each bar are now played to the time value of a crotchet, with a rest on beats 2 and 4 in the bar. While the pedal rests, the left hand chord is played to create an alternating movement between the pedal and the left hand chords. A play - release - play - release action for the pedal notes and a rest - play - rest - play action for the chords for each bar will help you to maintain the correct timing of the music.

Fig. 2 Pedal - chord - pedal - chord movement

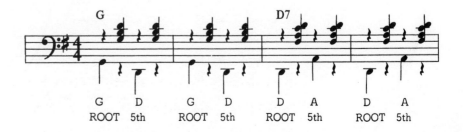

To develop a waltz rhythm technique, known as pedal - chord - chord accompaniment, the pedal note and left hand chords will each have the time value of a crotchet. The music will be written in ¾ time, three crotchet beats in each bar and in fig. 3 the music is written in the key of C major.

The pedal note, played on the first crotchet beat in the bar, is immediately released and will rest for the remainder of the bar. The left hand chord rests on the first beat and then is played on the second beat and repeated on the third beat in each bar.

The root and fifth pedal notes are alternating between bars in the pedal - chord - chord movement in fig. 3. The root pedal note of C in the first bar is followed by the fifth note of G in the second bar with the C major left hand chord. The root pedal note of G in the third bar is followed by the fifth note of D in the fourth bar with the G7 chord.

Fig. 3 Pedal - chord - chord accompaniment

A complete table of root & fifth notes from each chord

The root note is also the name of the chord. Simply follow the arrows below the bass pedal board for left foot movement.

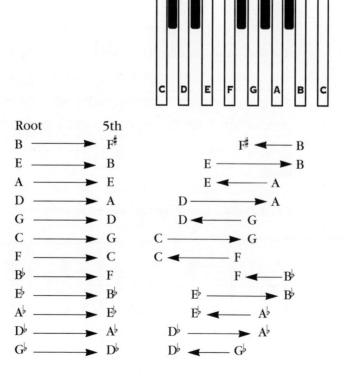

Root		5th			
B	→	F#		F# ←	B
E	→	B		E →	B
A	→	E		E ←	A
D	→	A	D →	A
G	→	D	D ←	G
C	→	G	C →	G
F	→	C	C ←	F
B♭	→	F		F ←	B♭
E♭	→	B♭	E♭ →	B♭
A♭	→	E♭	E♭ ←	A♭
D♭	→	A♭	D♭ →	A♭
G♭	→	D♭	D♭ ←	G♭

A latin rhythmic accompaniment to music written in $\frac{4}{4}$ time is shown in fig. 4. Counting 1 & 2 & 3 & 4 & for the eight quaver beats in each bar will help you to play this rhythm. The illustration is written in the key of F major. The pedal note of F played on the first beat, rests on the second crotchet beat in the bar and is then played again on the third and fourth beats. The root pedal note only is played for this rhythm.

Try to get the timing pattern of the left hand chords:

oom - pah h h - pah, oom - pah, oom - pah.

While oom is representing the pedal notes the pah accounts for the chords. The pah h h represents the first and only crotchet chord in the bar.

Fig. 4 Latin rhythm

The accompaniment technique for playing to a shuffle or western rhythm is illustrated in fig. 5. Count 1 & 2 & 3 & 4 & for each bar, just as for the latin rhythm. The pedal note, sounding on beats 1 and 3 will rest on beats 2 and 4 while the left hand chords are played. Again there is a variation in the chord note values. On the second beat in each bar the two quaver note chords are played quickly, one after the other. Try to achieve an oom - pah - pah, oom - pah effect of pedal - chord chord, pedal - chord in each bar.

Fig. 5 Shuffle or western rhythm

The baion left hand chord and bass pedal accompaniment is ideally suited to the modern slow beat rhythm. Root bass pedal notes only are played with the sustained left hand chords in fig. 6. The first pedal note in each bar with the time value of three quavers (a dotted crotchet) is followed by a quaver and crotchet pedal note before resting for the last crotchet beat in the bar.

Fig. 6 Baion bass pedal rhythm

Counting   1 & 2 & 3 & 4 & 1 & 2 & 3 & 4 & 1 & 2 & 3 & 4 &

Experiment with the various bass pedal rhythms when playing your own music and don't panic if the rhythm unit seems to run away from you. Simply adjust the speed and try again.

ALTERNATIVE BASS PEDAL NOTES

For the organist learning to play with chord symbols, instructions for playing an alternative pedal note to the root note normally played with each left hand chord will be written as the chord name followed by the pedal note name and divided by an oblique line, ie. a chord symbol of E♭/G represents the E♭ major chord played with a G pedal note. A chord symbol of F/A tells you to play the F major chord with an A pedal note etc.

The answer to the formation of E♭ chords from the E♭ major scale

E♭ major	1	-	3	-	5			
	E♭		G		B♭			

E♭ 6th	1	-	3	-	5	6		
	E♭		G		B♭	C		

E♭ 7th	1	-	3	-	5	-	7♭	
	E♭		G		B♭		D♭	

E♭ minor	1	-	3♭	-	5			
	E♭		G♭		B♭			

E♭ minor 6th	1	-	3♭	–	5	6		
	E♭		G♭		B♭	C		

E♭ minor 7th	1	-	3♭	-	5	-	7♭	
	E♭		G♭		B♭		D♭	

E♭ major 7th	1	-	3	-	5	-	7	
	E♭		G		B♭		D	

E♭ major 9th	1	-	3	-	5	-	7	-	9
	E♭	-	G	-	B♭	-	D	-	F

—— chord ——

E♭ 9th	1	-	3	-	5	-	7♭	–	9
	E♭	-	G	-	B♭	-	D♭	-	F

E♭ 11th	1	-	–	–	5	-	7♭	-	9	-	11
	E♭				B♭		D♭		F		A♭

——— chord ———

E♭ 13	1	-	–	–	–	–	7♭	8	-	10	-	-	13
	E♭						D♭	E♭		G			C

E♭ 13 (9)	1	-	–	–	–	–	7♭	-	9	10	-	-	13
	E♭						D♭		F	G			C

E♭ 13 (9 & 11)	1	-	–	–	–	–	7♭	-	9	-	11	-	13
	E♭						D♭		F		A♭		C

pedal   ——— chord ———

PART II
HARMONY

■ KEY SIGNATURES

As explained in Part I, a key signature consisting of sharps and flats, is written upon the staves after the treble and bass clef signs and represents a key of music.

The sharps and flats on the staves perform certain functions: they indicate which notes are to be sharpened or flattened throughout the music; and they are a signature for the particular key in which the music is written, in much the same way as we identify ourselves by our own personal signature.

A key of music revolves around a scale of music: the sharps or flats not only tell you which key you are playing in, but also represent the scale of the same name, which the composer or arranger used for writing the musical score.

Music written in the key of C major is easily recognisable by the absence of any sharps or flats in the key signature, as there are no sharps or flats in the C major scale:

C   D   E   F   G   A   B   C

Music written in the key of F major will have as a key signature a single flat ($\flat$) on the B line of the staves to represent the B$\flat$ note in the F major scale (the other seven notes are all natural notes):

F   G   A   B$\flat$ C   D   E   F

The B$\flat$ as a key signature, both tells you that you are playing in the key (and scale) of F major and instructs you to play any note of B in the music as B$\flat$.

The F major key signature & B$\flat$ notes on the treble & bass staves

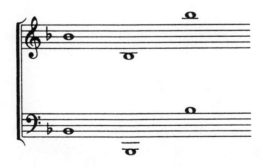

One more example of a key signature should clarify.

The three flats B$\flat$, E$\flat$ and A$\flat$ in the E$\flat$ major scale

E$\flat$ F   G   A$\flat$ B$\flat$ C   D   E$\flat$

will be written as a key signature to represent the key and scale of E$\flat$ major.

The notes B, E and A in the music will be played as flattened notes B♭, E♭ and A♭.

E♭ key signature & E♭ major scale

When a sharp or a flat not in the key signature precedes a note on the stave it is called an accidental and will sharpen or flatten the note it is written against. A natural sign (♮) placed before a note on the stave will cancel a sharpened or flattened note indicated by the key signature, or by a previous accidental.

You may already have seen a 'Circle of Keys' (fig. 1), but few keyboard players know how to interpret it or realise its significance. It displays keynotes and key signatures and is intended to be read in both a clockwise and anticlockwise direction. However, it seems complicated to use.

The Musical Ladder is adapted from the Circle of Keys, and while it contains exactly the same information it is much easier to use.

The circle has been turned around so that the F♯ and G♭ keynotes are at 6 o'clock and by opening the circle out the F♯ keynote is at the top of the ladder and the G♭ keynote is at the base of the ladder. The keynotes on the ladder follow the same sequences in an upward or downward direction, as when the circle is read in a clockwise or anticlockwise direction.

Figure. 1 Circle of Keys & Musical Ladder (adapted from the Circle of Keys)

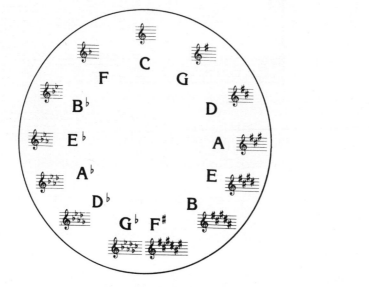

The Musical Ladder highlights how the sharps and flats from each major scale are placed upon the treble and bass staves to represent the key of the same name.

■ THE MUSICAL LADDER

KEY	Major Scales	Key Signatures	
F♯	F♯ G♯ A♯ B C♯ D♯ E♯ F♯		F♯ C♯ G♯ D♯ A♯ E♯
B	B C♯ D♯ E F♯ G♯ A♯ B		F♯ C♯ G♯ D♯ A♯
E	E F♯ G♯ A B C♯ D♯ E		F♯ C♯ G♯ D♯
A	A B C♯ D E F♯ G♯ A		F♯ C♯ G♯
D	D E F♯ G A B C♯ D		F♯ C♯
G	G A B C D E F♯ G		F♯
C	C D E F G A B C		
F	F G A B♭ C D E F		B♭
B♭	B♭ C D E♭ F G A B♭		B♭ E♭
E♭	E♭ F G A♭ B♭ C D E♭		B♭ E♭ A♭
A♭	A♭ B♭ C D♭ E♭ F G A♭		B♭ E♭ A♭ D♭
D♭	D♭ E♭ F G♭ A♭ B♭ C D♭		B♭ E♭ A♭ D♭ G♭
G♭	G♭ A♭ B♭ C♭ D♭ E♭ F G♭		B♭ E♭ A♭ D♭ G♭ C♭

On the Musical Ladder the eight notes of each major scale are written beside the keynote (also called the root note, or first note) of that scale. For instance, written beside the key note of D♭ are the eight notes of the D♭ major scale. The ladder also highlights how the sharps and flats from each major scale are written in their correct sequence on the treble and bass staves as a signature representing each major key of music.

When ascending the Musical Ladder from the key of C to the key of F♯, each key signature contains sharps, starting with the single F♯ representing the key of G major, through to the six sharps in the key of F♯ major. Each added sharp in each new key signature is the new sharpened note in each major scale: ie. key of G - F♯, key of D - F♯ and C♯, key of A - F♯, C♯ and G♯ and so on.

When descending the ladder from the key of C to the key of G♭, each key signature contains flats starting with the single B♭ representing the key of F major to the six flats representing the key of G♭ major. Each added flat in each new key signature is the new flattened note in each major scale: ie. key of F - B♭, key of B♭ - B♭ and E♭, key of E♭ - B♭, E♭ and A♭ and so on.

■ MAJOR SCALES, RELATIVE MINOR SCALES & CHORDS IN A KEY

Why do you need to know the key of the music you are playing in and how can that information help you to improve your playing?

In 'middle of the road' or 'standard' music, three basic chords belonging to each key will be written regularly throughout the arrangement and by being able to identify the key you are playing in, you will know which left hand chords you can expect to encounter in the music, which in turn encourages fluency of playing by smooth, positive finger movements between the chords.

As the three basic chords in each key of music will be formed upon specific notes of scale with the same name as the key, it is now necessary to learn the technical names of the eight notes of a scale.

1	2	3	4	5	6	7	8
Tonic (Root)	Super Tonic	Mediant	Sub Dominant	Dominant Fifth	Sub Mediant	Leading Note	Tonic

In each key of music the three basic chords are formed upon the tonic (or root note), the dominant fifth note and the subdominant fourth note of scale with the same name as the key. Take, as an example, an arrangement written in the key of C. To identify the three basic chords from the scale of C major, form a major chord upon the tonic note of C: C major. Form a seventh chord upon the dominant fifth note of G: G 7th. And form a major chord upon the subdominant note of F: F major.

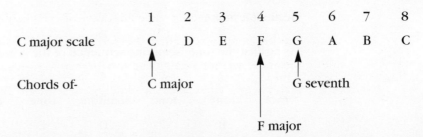

	1	2	3	4	5	6	7	8
C major scale	C	D	E	F	G	A	B	C
Chords of-	C major				G seventh			
				F major				

These three basic chords of C major, G 7th and F major will have consistently occurred in the first simple tunes that you have played, undoubtedly written in the key of C major.

There can be variations to the chords formed upon the tonic and subdominant fourth notes, such as sixth and minor sixth chords, but in the early stages of playing, the chord formed upon the dominant fifth note will be a seventh only and is known as the dominant seventh chord.

Additional left hand chords can, of course, be included in the music, formed from a key which is related to the major key you are playing in.

■ RELATIVE MINOR SCALES

The major key will have as a 'relative' a minor key. We have already established the link between the major key, major scale and the basic chords and by forming a minor scale we can find its three basic chords and therefore the additional chords in each key.

The last three notes of a major scale are the first three notes of its relative minor scale or, if it's easier for you to remember, the sixth note of a major scale is the first note of the relative minor scale. As with the major scale, the first note is also the root note of the minor scale. For example, the last three notes of the C major scale A, B and C are the first three notes of its relative minor scale, A:

	1	2	3	4	5	6	7	8
C major scale	C	D	E	F	G	A	B	C
A minor scale (first 3 notes)						A	B	C♮

The natural sign representing the C natural note must be included, as the third note of the A major scale is C♯. It is the third note of a scale which determines whether it is a major or minor.

Having established the rule for finding the first three notes of a relative minor scale, it only remains to find the remaining five notes of the scale. The tone semitone sequence of a minor scale differs from that of the major scale. The sequence for a minor scale is:

1	2	3	4	5	6	7	8
root	tone	semitone	tone	tone	semitone	tone & semitone	semitone

Scale of A minor

A B C♮ D E F♭ G♯ A

As against the tone, semitone sequence of the A major scale.

1	2	3	4	5	6	7	8
root	tone	tone	semitone	tone	tone	tone	semitone
A	B	C♯	D	E	F♯	G♯	A

In the minor scale formation there is a large gap between the sixth and seventh notes of scale (see the F♮ to G♯ in the A minor scale) but this is necessary in creating the harmony of the scale. The additional chords in a key of music can now be formed from the A minor scale in exactly the same way as the three basic chords were formed from the C major scale.

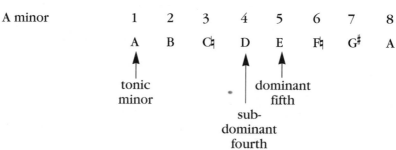

A minor

	1	2	3	4	5	6	7	8
	A	B	C♮	D	E	F♮	G♯	A

tonic minor — sub-dominant fourth — dominant fifth

Therefore, additional chords included in music written in the key of C major can be A minor (Am), formed upon the tonic note, D minor (Dm) formed upon the subdominant fourth note and E minor seventh (Em7) formed upon the dominant fifth note of the A minor scale. The chord names such as A, D and E are the most important factors rather than the possible variations (m), (m7) etc. of the chords.

When combined, the basic and additional chords in the key of C major are; C major, F major, (F6) or (Fm6), G 7th from the C major scale and A minor (Am7), D minor (Dm7) and E minor (Em7) from the relative A minor scale.

Further additional chords can occur in the music when, for example, there is a change of key for the middle eight bars, or for a whole section of the music. The key of music determines the accompanying chords but there are no hard and fast rules for the arranger's use of chords and their progressions. As I am teaching you the basic construction of harmony in music my methods can be applied for finding the chords within any key.

Music written in the key of E♭ major will contain the three basic chords of E♭ major, B♭ 7th and A♭ major formed upon the tonic, dominant fifth and subdominant 4th notes of the E♭ major scale.

Left hand chords in the key of E♭ major

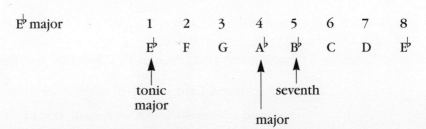

E♭ major	1	2	3	4	5	6	7	8
	E♭	F	G	A♭	B♭	C	D	E♭

tonic
major

major

seventh

Form the relative minor scale of C minor to find the additional chords in the key of E♭ major. The last three notes of the E♭ major scale - C, D and E♭ - are the first three notes of its relative minor scale (C minor).

The notes of the two related scales are:

E♭ major 1 2 3 4 5 6 7 8
      E♭ F G A♭ B♭ C D E♭

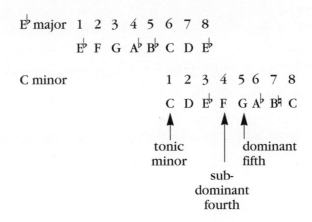

C minor

	1	2	3	4	5	6	7	8
	C	D	E♭	F	G	A♭	B♮	C

tonic
minor

dominant
fifth

sub-
dominant
fourth

The combined chords when playing in the key of E♭ major will be E♭ major formed upon the tonic, B♭ 7th formed upon the dominant fifth note and A♭ major formed upon the subdominant fourth note of the E♭ major scale. The additional chords are C minor (tonic), F minor (subdominant fourth) and G minor 7 (dominant fifth) from the related C minor scale, although variations of these chords, such as (6), (7th) etc. can occur in a major or minor form in the music.

The rules are now established for finding chords in any key.

Follow the steps below to find the left hand chords in a key of your choice in exactly the same way as for the two keys of C and E♭ major:

1. write the scale with the same name as the key

2. form the three basic chords

3. form the relative minor scale

4. find the three additional chords to combine them with the three basic chords of the related major key.

Refer to a favourite arrangement of your own to see the combination of chords within a key.

Each major scale and its relative minor scale

Major scale-	F♯	B	E	A	D	G	C	F	B♭	E♭	A♭	D♭	G♭
Relative minor scale	D♯m	G♯m	C♯m	F♯m	Bm	Em	Am	Dm	Gm	Cm	Fm	B♭m	E♭m

On the Musical Ladder you will see that the keynotes naming the combined basic and additional chords within one key are in a sequence on the ladder in the immediate vicinity of the home keynote (which is the key you are playing in). For instance, playing in the key of C major, the combined keynote chord names of E, A, D, G, C and F within this key are four steps up the ladder from the home keynote of C and also one step down.

Key	Key of C major	Key of E♭ major
F♯		
B		
E	E (m) (7)	
A	A (m) (7)	
D	D (m) (7)	
G	G (7 only)	G (m)
C	C home keynote	C (m) (7)
F	F (m) (m6)	F (m) (7)
B♭		B♭ (7 only)
E♭		E♭ home keynote
A♭		A♭ (m) (6)
D♭		
G♭		

When playing in the key of E♭ major, the six keynote sequence of chords on the ladder are four steps up from the home keynote of E♭ and also one step down.

Music can also be written in a minor key which can initially escape the attention of the organist, as the key signature will appear to be representing the relative major key. For instance, the key of A minor will have the same key signature as its related key of C major, with a noticeable absence of any sharps or flats.

Identical key signatures of C major & A minor

The left hand chords belonging to the minor key and appearing regularly throughout the music will now be in sequence on the ladder in the immediate vicinity of the minor home keynote of A rather than its related major home keynote of C.

Left hand chord sequences on the musical ladder in the keys of C major and A minor

Key	Key of C major	Key of A minor
F$^\sharp$		F$^\sharp$ (m)
B		B (m) (7)
E	E (m)	E (7 only)
A	A (m) (7)	Am home keynote
D	D (m) (7)	D (m) (m6)
G	G (7 only)	
C	C home keynote	
F	F (m) (m6)	
B$^\flat$		
E$^\flat$		
A$^\flat$		
D$^\flat$		
G$^\flat$		

Left hand chords in a minor key will not always be in a minor form and will not necessarily be written in their sequence on the ladder. As minor chords occur in a major key, so major chords will be played in a minor key.

Example of left hand chords in C major

Example of left hand chords in the related key of A minor

The key of C minor will have the same key signature of three flats - B$^\flat$, E$^\flat$ and A$^\flat$ - as its related key, E$^\flat$ major.

Identical key signatures of E♭ major & C minor

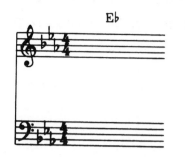

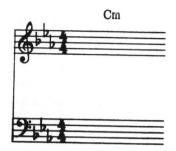

Left hand chord sequences on the Musical Ladder in the keys of E♭ major and C minor

Key	Key of E♭ major	Key of C minor
F♯		
B		
E		E (m)
A		A (m) (7)
D		D (m) (7)
G	G (m)	G (7)
C	C (m) (7)	Cm home keynote
F	F (m) (7)	F (m) (6)
B♭	B♭ (7)	
E♭	E♭ home keynote	
A♭	A♭ (m) (6)	
D♭		
G♭		

Example of left hand chords in E♭ major

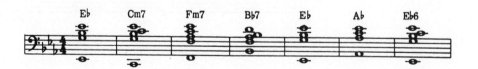

Example of left hand chords in the related key of C minor

Music written in a minor key will normally have a sad sound, just as when a minor chord is compared with a major chord. See if you can find one of your own arrangements written in a minor key. To help you, the music will usually start and end on a minor chord and the chord sequences in the music will be mainly in a minor form.

■ INTERVALS

Left hand chords contain notes at various intervals to each other and the combination of intervals within a chord determine the right type of chords to use in a chord progression.

The following table shows the intervals within the octave and will apply to all major keys of music.

C to D is a Major Second	C to D♭ is a Minor Second
C to E is a Major Third	C to E♭ is a Minor Third
C to F is a Perfect 4th	C to F♭ is a Diminished 4th
C to G is a Perfect 5th	C to G♭ is a Diminished 5th
C to A is a Major 6th	C to A♭ is a Minor 6th
C to B is a Major 7th	C to B♭ is a Minor 7th
C to C is a Perfect Octave	C to C♭ is a Diminished Octave

Intervals of music are reckoned by the number of note names in a consecutive sequence inclusive of the upper and lower notes. C to E is an interval of a third because it uses three note names: C - D - E. C to G is an interval of a fifth because there are five note names in the sequence: C - D - E - F - G.

Briefly, there are two forms of intervals in the make-up of a chord which create the musical effects that you hear:

1. consonant intervals: these intervals can be perfect and imperfect. The perfect consonant intervals are the perfect fourth, perfect fifth and octave and the imperfect consonant intervals are the major and minor third, major and minor sixth and the major seventh.

2. dissonant intervals: these intervals are the major second and minor seventh.

Musical intervals make up two types of chord - concord and discord. Chords in the concord group contain the perfect and imperfect consonant intervals. The chords of major, minor, major and minor sixth, major and minor seventh containing these intervals do not need to be followed by another chord in the music (called a resolution) as their notes combine in an agreement of sound and the chords are complete and final in themselves.

Play this group of concord chords:

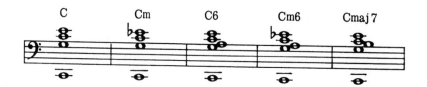

Chords in the discord group contain one or more dissonant intervals. The seventh, ninth, eleventh and thirteenth chords containing these intervals do require a resolution as their combination of notes create a restless sound, always needing to move on to another chord.

Play this group of discord chords:

Prove this point by playing a concord such as C major or C6 which does not require a resolution followed by a discord such as G7 to hear the effect of a need for movement, or resolution, to a concord, in this instance (example 1) C major.

Example 1

Play example 2 to hear the discord B♭7, needing to resolve to the E♭ major chord.

Example 2

The next section shows you how the sequences of concord and discord chords combine in written music.

■ HARMONY

So what is harmony? In its basic form it is a method of chord construction by intervals of music and also chord formation in relation to a scale already discussed in this book.

Harmony is also the relationship of successive chords to each other, known as harmonic chord sequences, harmonic chord progressions, or simply a sequence of left hand chords in harmony. You will have already played basic chord progressions such as C to F to G7 to C in your first simple tunes, which were adequate to accompany the melody and sparsely written in the music.

The Musical Ladder forms the basis for creating left hand chord progressions, by playing each keynote as a major chord followed by the same chord with a seventh note added.

Start at the top of the Musical Ladder to play an F# chord. Add a seventh note of E and play the F#7 chord to its resolution of B, one step down the ladder. Add the seventh note of A to the B chord to play the B7 chord to its resolution of E.

Continue to move down the ladder, one step at a time, playing each keynote chord followed by the same chord with a seventh note added to it until you reach the last keynote chord of G♭, when you will be back at the starting point of F# (G♭ enharmonic).

Write out the remaining ladder chord progression (following illustration) on the manuscript.

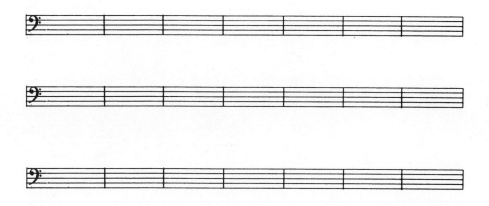

When you first start to play the sequence of major and seventh chords from F♯ to G♭ you will probably be too absorbed in finding the notes of each chord to hear the harmony you are creating. Once you have achieved smooth finger movements to fluently play the sequence, tape yourself and listen to the full effect of the harmonic chord progression. You may recognise familiar groups of chord in the sequence which have consistently occurred in music you have been playing and relate to the previous chords in a key section.

The table of left hand chord progressions on the Musical Ladder from F♯ to G♭ shows how each chord can be played between the octave F to F (on the lower manual of a dual manual organ) to ensure a smooth movement between chords. The root note of each chord is played as the pedal note. One note only is written beside each seventh chord which is added to the preceding major chord.

Keynotes	F	G	A	B	C	D	E	F
F♯	F♯	–	A♯	–	C♯			
F♯ 7							E	
B	F♯	–	–	B	–	D♯		
B7			A					
E		G♯	–	B	–	–	E	
E7						D		
A			A	–	C♯	–	E	
A7		G						
D		F♯	–	A	–	–	D	
D7					C			
G		G	–	B	–	D		
G7								F
C		G	–	–	C	–	E	
C7				B♭				
F		F	–	A	–	C		
F7							E♭	
B♭		F	–	–	B♭	–	D	
B♭7			A♭					
E♭		G	–	B♭	–	–	E♭	
E♭7						D♭		
A♭			A♭	–	C	–	E	
A♭7		G♭						
D♭		F	–	A♭	–	–	D♭	
D♭7				B				
G♭		G♭	–	B♭	–	D♭		

As illustrated by the chord progression on the ladder, a seventh chord opens a door to another chord. In your own music you can see for yourself how chord progressions occur, ie G7 to C, B♭7 to E♭, A♭7 to D♭ etc.

Minor seventh chords lead smoothly and in harmony to a seventh chord, followed by a major or major sixth chord. The minor seventh chord does not move smoothly to a major chord (broken harmony) but needs the inclusion of a seventh chord for a complete harmony movement.

Play the following examples to hear how the F♯m7 chord does not move smoothly to the E major chord (broken harmony) as it does when the B7 chord is included (harmony). Refer to the Musical Ladder to see that when each keynote is used in a downward movement, the smooth effect of harmony is achieved.

Example 1 Broken harmony

Broken harmony

F♯m7

  ?

E

Harmony

F♯m7

  B7

   E

The inclusion of the B7 chord between the F♯m7 and E chords completes the harmony movement.

Starting with the keynote of A on the ladder, play the Am7 chord followed by the G major chord. Notice that the D7th chord is missing. As the keynote and therefore the chord of D was omitted the smooth chord progression was lost.

Example 2 Broken harmony

Broken harmony

A m7

  ?

G

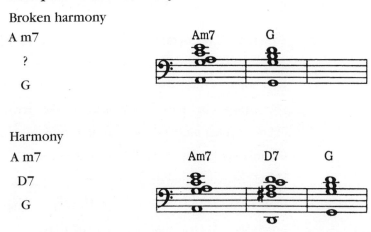

Harmony

A m7

  D7

   G

The inclusion of the D7th chord completes the harmony movement between the Am7 and G chords.

The minor seventh chord will also move smoothly to another minor seventh chord:

A m7

Dm7

G7

C

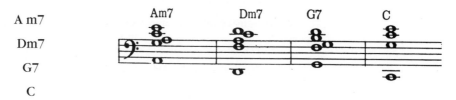

or you can 'mix and match' the minor seventh and seventh chords in the progression, providing that the seventh chord only moves to the major chord.

One more example of the Musical Ladder chord progression:

A m7

D7

G7

C

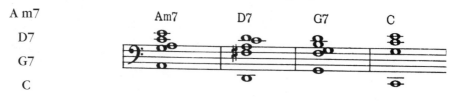

C m7

Fm7

B♭7

E♭

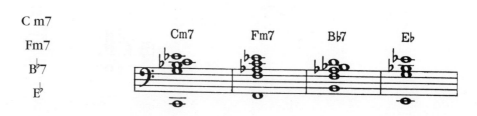

The chord progressions will depend upon the type of music being played and, of course, the melody line.

Try to memorise the sequence of the Musical Ladder. Starting at the top, F#️ followed by the word BEAD. G, C and F are next before the word BEAD again, this time with a ♭ beside each letter, B♭ E♭ A♭ and D♭, and lastly the G♭ at the base.

F#️   B   E   A   D   G   C   F   B♭   E♭   A♭   D♭   G♭

■ ADDING LEFT HAND CHORDS TO YOUR OWN MUSIC

Find some of your own music to identify the chord progressions. Some of your first simple musical arrangements are written with very few left hand chords, which are held for a number of bars making the accompaniment to the melody line static and devoid of interest. You can learn to fill in added chords by cultivating finger movement only, to form additional chords of the same name as the chord symbol, to adapt a single major chord into a chord progression such as maj7 to 6 to maj7 to 6 etc.

A single chord of C major covering a number of bars of music can be adapted to Cmaj7 - C6 - Cmaj7 - C6 to create a chord progression.

Starting with the C major chord, hold on to the three notes, G - - C - E, add the note B to play the C major seventh chord. To play the C6 chord omit the B note and add the A note, still holding on to the three original notes. Return to the C major seventh chord by omitting the A note and adding the B note, then omit the B note to play the C major chord.

Look at the finger movement between the chords on the manual.

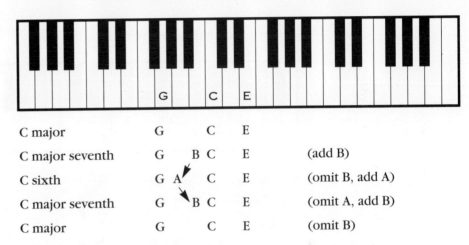

C major	G		C	E	
C major seventh	G	B	C	E	(add B)
C sixth	G A		C	E	(omit B, add A)
C major seventh	G	B	C	E	(omit A, add B)
C major	G		C	E	(omit B)

Fingers 5(G), 2(C) and the thumb (E) remain static throughout the C chord progression, formed from the single C major chord. Use fingers three and four for the moving notes B to A to B. The C pedal note can be sustained throughout the chord progression or played with each chord.

Your music could be written like this with a single chord of C held for two bars:

and be played like this, with finger movement creating a C chord progression from the single chord of C major:

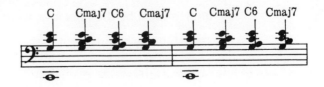

Your music could contain a single chord of F major held for two bars:

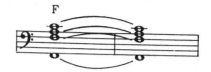

and played as a chord progression of F from the single F major chord.

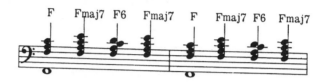

Below is shown finger movement on the manual.

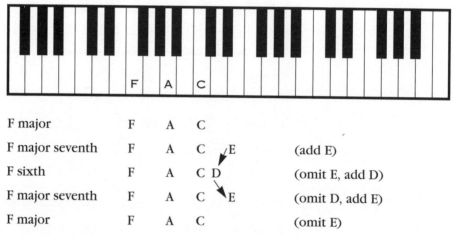

F major	F	A	C	
F major seventh	F	A	C ⟋E	(add E)
F sixth	F	A	C D	(omit E, add D)
F major seventh	F	A	C ↘E	(omit D, add E)
F major	F	A	C	(omit E)

Fingers 5(F), 4(A) and 2(C) remain still throughout the F chord progression formed from the single F major chord, while the thumb moves between the notes of E and D.

When you are listening to an orchestra, or a group of musicians, have you ever shut out the melody and concentrated on what is actually being played as the accompaniment or backing? If you have, part of the effects you hear are harmony created by chord progressions, as the musicians are not all playing the melody line.

A piece of music is divided into parts and shared amongst the musicians to be blended together into a complete melodious arrangement. You can now use the chord progressions sparingly to help you, the versatile solo keyboard player, to produce similar effects to those groups of musicians. And 'sparingly' should be the operative word, as over-use of chord progressions can create too much movement in the accompaniment.

■ MELODY NOTES HELPING TO CREATE CHORD PROGRESSIONS

The melody notes in music can help to determine which chords will fill-in the spaces, as they are often the notes which can be added to the single left hand chord to play extra chords of the same name.

In the first example, below, the bar of music is written with a single left hand chord of F major and the three melody notes of E, D and C. The E melody note is a guide for substituting the Fmaj7 chord with the notes F - A - C - E for the F major chord. Similarly, the next melody note in the bar, D, can be added to the F major chord to play F6; F - A - C D. The last melody note in the bar, C, is a note from the F major chord, completing the bar naming the original chord of the music.

The second example shows the melody notes of E and D added to the left hand major chord of F to produce the chord progression of Fmaj7, F6 and F major within the bar.

Example 1

Melody notes E   D   C

Example 2

Chord progression; Fmaj7 : F–A–C–E*

Melody notes*   F6   : F–A–C D*

added to left   F   : F–A–C

hand chord

The following example shows the same movement with a G major chord and the melody notes of F♯ and E, used to create additional left hand chords included in the bar.

Example 3

Melody notes F♯ E D

Example 4

Chord progression;	Gmaj7	: G–B–D–F♯*
Melody notes*	G6	: G–B–DE*
added to left	G	: G–B–D
hand chord		

The G major chord becomes Gmaj7 when the F♯ melody note is added and G6 when the E melody note is added. The melody note of D is a note of the original G major chord in the music.

A sound knowledge of the notes in each left hand chord is essential if you are hoping to embellish your own music this way. See if you can identify those melody notes in your own music which can be added to a single left hand chord to form additional fill-in chords to play as a chord progression.

Now that you have learned harmony movement between the major seventh, sixth and major chords and also chord progressions on the Musical Ladder, you can use them to embellish a simple musical arrangement.

The 'original' following example contains the F major chord to be played for two bars, a C7 chord for the next two bars, before returning to the F major chord for the last bar (example 5). You can now create an accompaniment movement by chord additions and chord substitution. See the 'embellished' example 6.

Example 5 Original

Example 6 Embellished

In the first two bars of the embellished example, the Fmaj7 and F6 chords have been substituted for the sustained F major chord in the original example. In the third bar, the C7 chord has been replaced completely by the Gm7 chord (one step up the ladder), creating a harmony movement to lead smoothly into the C7 chord in the fourth bar, before resolving to the F major chord in the last bar.

■ BASS PEDAL PROGRESSIONS

Following the subject of left hand chord progressions, this seems to be the appropriate place to include bass pedal progressions, which can be used as an alternative to rhythmic bass pedal techniques discussed later.

A pedal progression is a movement in harmony from one pedal note to another, which can be achieved even though you are reading chord symbols, when normally the root note only of an accompanying chord is played, or when the music contains a very sparsely written bass stave.

To embellish, or add to basic bass stave notation, extra pedal notes can be slotted in between a single pedal note in two consecutive bars of music, so that any silence or spaces between the pedal notes are filled in.

I must first establish that any added notes to fill the spaces are completely dependent upon the key or scale in which the music is written.

For the first pedal fill-in I will use the last two bars of a simple arrangement in the key of C major containing a G7 chord (G pedal) in the last bar but one, followed by the C major chord (C pedal) in the last bar (example 7).

The fill-in notes will move in a downward direction on the pedal board from the single G pedal note to the C pedal note in the last bar while the timing of the music is maintained.

Playing in the key of C major, which also represents the scale of C major, the single pedal note of G, fifth note of the C major scale, can be followed by the fourth note of F, third note of E, and second note of D (from the same scale), before finally moving to the first, or root note of C in the last bar. A simple pedal progression of G to F to E to D to C, fifth to root note of the C major scale or key that you are playing in (example 7a).

Example 7 The last two bars in the key of C major

Example 7a The same bars with fill-in notes added

You can now use this simple pedal progression in any key using five to one of the scale with the same name as the key you are playing in.

Playing in the key of F major, the last two bars will contain the chords of C7 and F major and the pedal progression will be formed between the two single pedal notes of C and F accompanying the chords (example 8).

In this instance, the upper C pedal note should be played to allow for the downward movement to the F pedal note. The progression is from the C note accompanying the C7th chord to the final pedal note of F played with the last chord of F major, using the note sequence of C (5), B♭ (4), A (3) and G (2) before moving to the root note of F (1) of the F major scale (example 8a).

Example 8 As written in the music

Example 8a With fill-in notes added

The next subject, right hand chords, requires recognition of chord inversions. The following should help to quickly refresh your memory: to play a three note chord such as G major as an inversion, the root note of G is moved from the extreme left of the chord to the extreme right. This movement creates a first inversion. To create a second inversion move the note of B from the extreme left of the chord to the extreme right of the chord. With only three initial notes to move around there are only two possible inversions.

Chord Inversions (major chord)

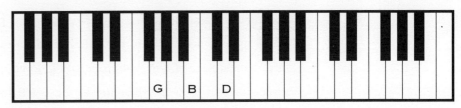

G major   G – B – D

1st inversion   B – D – – G

2nd inversion   D – – G – B

With a seventh chord, or any other chord of four notes, there are three possible inversions, but the movement remains the same.

Chord Inversions (7th chord)

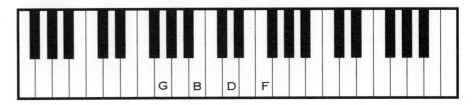

G seventh   G – B – D – F♯

1st inversion   B – D – F♯ G

2nd inversion   D – F♯ G – B

3rd inversion   F♯ G – B – D

Remember, only one note changes its position for each chord inversion

■ RIGHT HAND CHORDS

In this section I would like to look at right hand chords. A clue to solving the mystery that surrounds them is the fact that a right hand chord will have the same name as the left hand chord with which it is being played.

Identifying chord inversions will help you to add a correct sequence of added notes to a single melody note to play a right hand chord containing the same notes as the left hand chord. A single melody note will be played as the dominant, highest note in the right hand chord and any added notes will be played underneath it.

The following illustrations show you how the single melody notes are played, with the duplicated notes of the left hand chords to form right hand chords.

In the first illustration you will be playing a right hand chord of C with the C major left hand chord. Abbreviations are used above the treble stave for a single melody note (SMN) and right hand chord (RHC) in each bar.

Your right hand is playing a single melody note of C, your left hand is playing a C major chord and you are playing a C pedal note. Underneath the single melody note of C in the first bar add the nearest note of G and the next nearest note of E in that order, going down the manual to play the same three notes of C, G and E as are in the C left hand chord. The right hand chord of C is an inversion of the left hand chord of C.

Illustration 1

In the second bar of illustration 1 the single melody note (SMN) of E will be played as a right hand chord of C when the notes of C and G, in that order, are added underneath the melody note of E.

In the third bar of the first illustration the single melody note of G will be played as a right hand chord of C when the notes of E and C are added underneath the melody note of G.

Illustration 2 shows you the make-up of right hand chords of F played with the left hand chord of F major and the F pedal note. The single melody notes are: bar 1, F; bar 2, C; bar 3, A. And each right hand chord of F will include the other two notes, duplicated from the left hand chord of F major.

Illustration 2

In illustration 3, the right hand chords of G7 are again formed with the single melody note and duplicated notes from the G7 left hand chord. The single melody notes are F (bar 1), D (bar 2), B (bar 3) and G (bar 4) and each right hand chord of G7 includes the duplicated notes of the G7 left hand chord. Contrast the right and left hand chords of G7 to clearly see the chord inversions.

Illustration 3

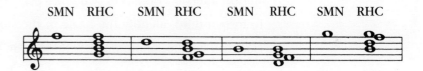

On a dual manual organ, right hand chords should be played an octave higher than normal on the upper manual to avoid a very muddy bass sound for the melody of the music. When playing in the 8va position, the dominant sounding melody note can be clearly heard above the agreement of sound created by the added notes which make up the right hand chord.

The rule is now established for identifying the notes of the left hand chord which can be duplicated and added to the single melody note to play a right hand chord. Initially, play the melody notes of longer time value, such as the semibreve, dotted minim, or minim, as right hand chords.

The simple tune of 'Plaisir D'Amour' is ideal as a starting point.

Illustration 4 'Plaisir D'Amour' with single melody notes

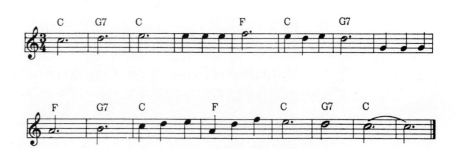

Illustration 5 'Plaisir D'Amour' with right hand chords

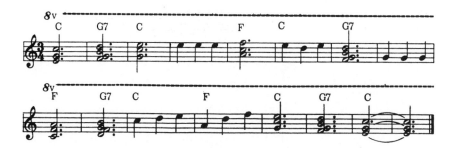

Play the music an octave higher on the upper manual of a dual manual organ than single melody notes.

■ THIRDS

Another method of creating a fuller, more interesting sound than playing single melody notes is by adding thirds. A third, which is also the term for a musical interval, consists of two notes played together as a right hand chord To form a third, identify the name of the single melody note in the music. This then becomes note number three in an alphabetical sequence of three notes. Note number one in the sequence of the three notes is added to and played underneath the single melody note, forming the third, while the second note in the sequence is ignored.

Examples 1, 2, 3 on the manual

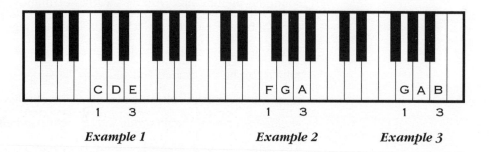

Example 1   *Example 2*   *Example 3*

In fig. 1 identify the first single melody note of E. Add the alphabetical note names prior to E (3) - D (2) and C (1) - to form the three note sequence. Only note no. 3 and note no. 1 are used to play the first third of E and C in fig. 2. Remember, the added note of C is played underneath the melody note The second melody note in fig. 1 is F and by adding the note no. in the alphabetical sequence - F (3), E (2), D (1) - to the melody note the second third of F and D is formed in fig. 2.

The third melody note of G, in fig. 1, will become a third by the addition of note no. 1 in the three note sequence of G (3), F (2), E (1). This third, in fig. 2, contains the notes of G and E.

Fig. 1

Melody notes   E F G

Fig. 2

Melody notes(3) E   F   G

Added notes(1)   C   D E

As the music in fig.s 3 and 4 is written in the key of C major, the C major scale will be used for identifying the thirds played in this key. C and E, D and F, E and G etc.

3rds in the C major scale

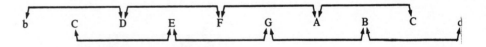

Fig. 3 A single melody line with accompanying chords

Now refer to fig. 4 to see the inclusion of the added note (no. 1) to form the thirds in each bar.

Fig. 4 3rds formed from single melody notes

Melody notes (3) E F G   C D E   A B C   F G A B

Added notes (1) C D E   A B C   F G A   D E F G

The left hand chords will have an influence upon the added notes played in the thirds. Playing in the key of C major, the chords of C major (Am7, Dm7 and G7) do not contain any sharpened or flattened notes, so the thirds are all formed from the natural notes; E and C, F and D, G and E etc.

If the Am7 chord (G A - C♮ - E) in the second bar of fig. 4 was replaced by the A7 chord (G A - C♯ - E), the first melody note in the bar would be C♯ instead of C♮, but the added note no. 1 would still be A, so the first third would be the notes of C♯ (3) and A (1). However, the third melody note of E in the same bar would need a C♯ note added to it to complete the third of E (3) and C♯ (1), because of the C♯ in the left hand chord of A7 (fig.s 5 and 6).

Fig. 5

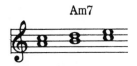

Am7

Melody notes(3)   C♮   D   E
Added notes(1)   A   B   C♮

Fig. 6

A7

Melody notes(3)   C♯   D   E
Added notes(1)   A   B   C♯

If the Dm7 chord (F♮ - A - C D) in the third bar of fig. 4 was replaced by the D7 chord (F♯ - A - C D) the added note no. 1 to form the first third in the bar would be F♯ instead of F♮ because of the F♯ note in the D7 chord as opposed to the F♮ note in the Dm7 chord (fig.s 7 and 8).

Fig. 7

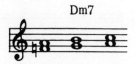

Dm7

Melody notes(3)   A   B   C
Added notes(1)   F♮ G   A

Fig. 8

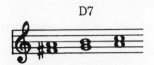

Melody notes(3) A   B   C

Added notes(1)   F# G   A

Do not forget that the notes added to create the thirds are played underneath the melody notes.

Study the illustrations of thirds in the E♭ major scale before playing the single melody notes in fig. 9 and the example in fig. 10 of added notes creating the fuller, more interesting sound of thirds in the key of E♭ major. The left hand chords of E♭, Cm7, Fm7 and B♭7 include the flattened notes to be played in the thirds.

3rds in the E♭ major scale

Fig. 9 Single melody notes

Fig. 10 Added 3rds

Melody notes (3)

      G A♭ B♭   E♭ F G   C D E♭   A♭ B♭ C D

Added notes

     E♭ F G   C D E♭   A♭ B♭ C   F G A♭ B♭

You can now embellish your own music with thirds in any key by following the simple established rules:

1. identify the key of the music you are going to play

2. write the scale of the same name as the key and link together the thirds in it

3. recognise the single melody note as the third note in an alphabetical sequence of three notes and add note no. 1 of each sequence to the single melody note (3) to create a third.

Write the added notes in pencil on the treble stave of your music so that you can erase any mistakes.

■ FINGERING

It is important to use the correct fingering for a smooth change between each third to allow the music to flow. Use a finger number sequence of 1 & 3, 2 & 4, 3 & 5 for the group of thirds in each bar. Fingers 1 & 3 for the first third, 2 & 4 for the second third and 3 & 5 for the third third in each bar.

■ CONCLUSION

No doubt you will recognise the embellishments of left hand chord progressions, thirds and right hand chords which I have added to the following, original arrangement of "Londonderry Air".

The left hand chord progression, formed from the single C major chord, C - Cmaj7 - C6 - Cmaj7 - C, is highlighted in bars four to five, and twelve to thirteen, while in bars two and twenty the added chords of Gmaj7 to G6 to G are formed from the single chord of G major. Notes added to the single melody note in many bars from thirds and right hand chords have been added discreetly.

The Musical Ladder progressions of chords-in-a-key occur as Am7 - D7 - G(maj7) in bars eight, nine and ten, and Am7 - D7($\flat$9) - G - C in bars fifteen and sixteen of the music.

The progressions of a seventh chord leading to a major chord, such as D7 or D7($\flat$9) to G and G7 to C are to be found in the music.

Listen to the harmony created by the additional melody notes in the thirds and right hand chords and the smooth, moving left hand chords by first playing the original arrangement, followed by the embellished version.

LONDONDERRY AIR

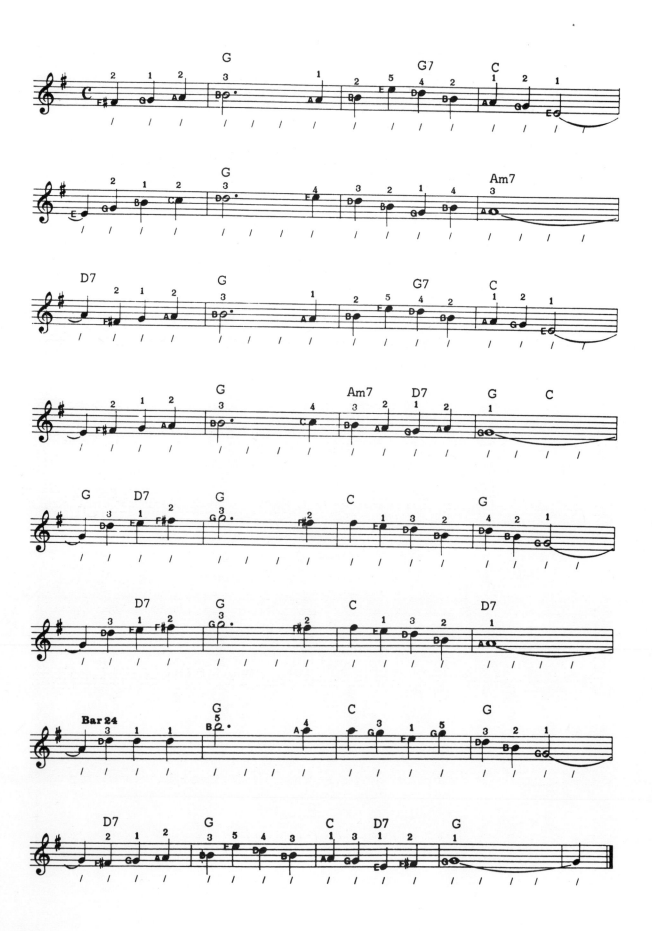

LONDONDERRY AIR

PART III
THE
PROFESSIONAL
TOUCH

■ TRANSPOSITION

Most musicians start to play in the two keys of C and F major and may feel that these two keys are adequate. They can be.

But to the listener with a good musical ear the music can all sound the same, despite variations in melody.

Transposition in relation to music simply means to change from one musical key to another. Learning how to transpose a favourite, well-played tune into another key can create new interest and a great sense of achievement.

Professional musicians can often transpose on sight, but unless musically gifted this can take quite a while to achieve.

There are various ways of transposing music. One method is to establish the tone and semitone distances between the original key and the new key and move every note accordingly, ie. when transposing from the key of F major to E♭ major there is a one tone distance in a downward movement. Every note on the original manuscript must be moved down by a tone distance on the new manuscript. This can be a complicated exercise if every note has to be moved by greater tone and semitone distances,which is the case between other major keys.

Using the major scales illustrated below it will be possible to transpose any of your favourite music, written in very simple keys, that you have mastered and discarded, or music written in difficult, unfamiliar keys that you would like to play.

My simple method of transposition is ideally suited for music written with a single treble stave and chord symbols, but I will also be showing you how to transpose and write the bass stave. All you require is a sheet of manuscript, a clean sheet of paper and a pen.

There are three main steps in preparation for transposition. They are as follows:

1. use a clean sheet of paper to write and number the eight notes of the scale with the same name as the key to be transposed.

2. write the eight notes of the scale representing the new key.

3. prepare the new manuscript by dividing it into bars and entering the key signature and time signature of the new key.

The first transposition will be "Plaisir D'Amour", written in the key of C major and transposed into the new key of E♭ major.

Step 1; on the clean sheet of paper write numbers 1 to 8 and directly below write the eight notes of the scale of C major, original key of C major (fig. 1a and 1b).

Step 2; write the scale of the new key, in this example E♭, directly underneath the eight notes of the C major scale

Figure 1a)	1	2	3	4	5	6	7	8
Figure 1b)	C	D	E	F	G	A	B	C
Figure 1c)	E♭	F	G	A♭	B♭	C	D	E♭

Step 3; on the new manuscript write in the new key signature, showing the three flats, B♭, E♭ and A♭, to represent the new key of E♭ major. Add the ¾ time signature.

Treble & bass staves in original key of C major & new key of E♭ major

Original key C major

New key E♭ major

You are now ready to start transposing from the key of C major to the new key of E♭ major by identifying each melody note as a number of the scale of the original key and then locating the corresponding note number of the new scale for the new key.

For example, in the following illustration, the note of C in the first bar of the original music is the first note of the C major scale. The corresponding first note of the E♭ major scale, E♭, will be written on the new manuscript as the first note in the first bar of the new key.

In the second bar of "Plaisir D'Amour" the note of D, second note of the C major scale, becomes the note F, second note of the E♭ major scale.

In the third and fourth bars, the notes of E (third note of the original scale of C) becomes the note of G (third note of the new scale of E♭).

Original key of C major

1st bar   2nd bar   3rd bar   4th bar

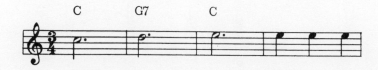

New key of E♭ major

The timing of the original music must be maintained, so ensure that all the notes and rests (if any) are transferred correctly.

To transpose the accompanying left hand chords, identify the chord symbol name as a note number of the original scale and then locate the corresponding note in the new key, in the same way that the melody notes were transposed.

For instance, a chord of C, note number one of the C major scale in the original key becomes the chord symbol E♭ note number one of the E♭ major scale in the new key of E♭ major. A chord symbol of G in the original key, fifth note of the C major scale, becomes B♭, fifth note of the E♭ major scale in the new key. All instructions following the name of the chord symbol, such as (7), (m7), (6) etc. must also be transferred from the original music to the new manuscript, ie. the chord symbol of G7 in the second bar of the original music becomes B♭7 in the second bar of the new manuscript.

For organists reading the bass stave, the left hand chords and bass pedal notes will be transposed by identifying each individual note as a note of the original scale of C major and then locating the corresponding note in the new scale of E♭ major.

The notes of the first chord of C major, G(5) - - C(1) - E(3) become B♭(5) - - E♭(1) - G(3) for the new chord of E♭. This chord will need to be inverted to be played between the octave F to F on a lower manual (G - B♭ - - E♭).

The notes of the G7 chord in the original manuscript G(1) - B(3) - D(5) - F(7♭) become B♭(1) - D(3) F(5) - A♭(7♭) on the new manuscript (B♭7 chord) needing to be inverted (A♭ - B♭ - D - F), before returning to the C chord original key, E♭ new key, for the third and fourth bars.

Bass staves in the keys of C major & E♭ major

Original key of C major

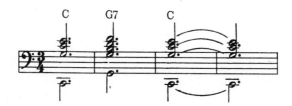

New key of E♭ major

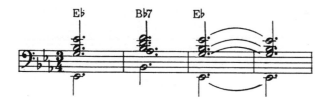

Transposing the bass stave is a time consuming effort when compared with the speedy transposition of chord symbols. By learning to name a group of notes written on the bass stave as a chord, a considerable amount of time can be saved when composing embellishments to music.

The following arrangement of "Plaisir D'Amour" is written with a time signature of ¾ and includes the bass stave in the key of C major so that you can compare it with the transposed arrangement below in the key of E♭ major.

PLAISIR D'AMOUR
IN THE KEY OF C MAJOR

PLAISIR D'AMOUR
IN THE KEY OF E♭ MAJOR

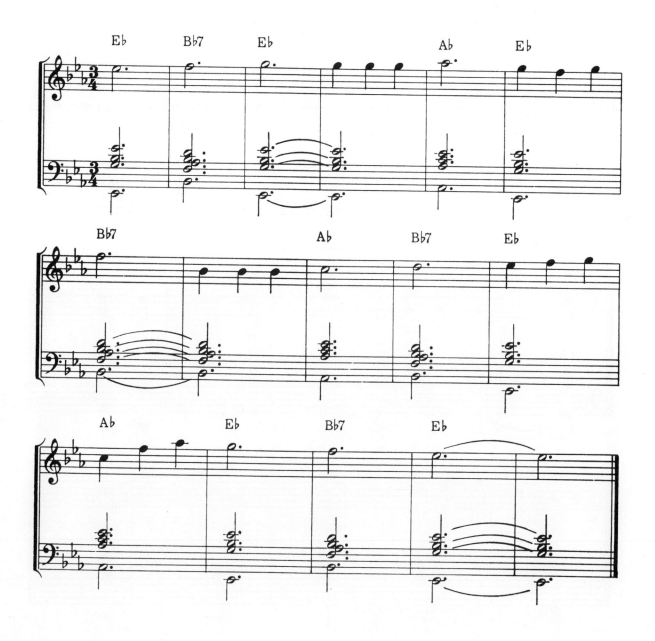

The rule for easy transposition is now established and following the three steps we will now transpose from the key of E♭ major into the new key of F major.

Step 1; write down and number 1 to 8 the notes of the E♭ major scale (original key).

Step 2; directly underneath the eight notes of the E♭ major scale write in the notes of the F major scale (new key).

Figure 1a)	1	2	3	4	5	6	7	8
Figure 1b)	E♭	F	G	A♭	B♭	C	D	E♭
Figure 1c)	F	G	A	B♭	C	D	E	F

Step 3; on the new manuscript write in the new key signature of B♭ to represent the new key of F major and write in the time signature of ¾.

Original key E♭ major

New key F major

To transpose "Santa Lucia" from the key of E♭ major into the new key of F major, identify each melody note as a number of the E♭ scale before locating the corresponding note numbers of the F major scale for the new key of F major.

Original key E♭ major

New key F major

Melody notes

Original Key E♭   New Key F

Bar 1	-	B♭(5)	E♭(8)	⟶	C(5)	F(8)
Bar 2	-	E♭(8)	D(7)	⟶	F(8)	E(7)
Bar 3	-	A♭(4)	C(6)	⟶	B♭(4)	D(6)
Bar 4	-	C(6)	B♭(5)	⟶	D(6)	C(5)

Now transpose the accompanying chords whether using chord symbols or the bass stave.

The first chord symbol of E♭, first note of the E♭ major scale becomes the chord symbol of F, first note of the F major scale in the new key. In the second and third bars the chord symbol of B♭(7), fifth note of the E♭ major scale, becomes C(7), fifth note of the F major scale, before returning to the chord of E♭, original key, and F, new key in the fourth bar.

To transpose the bass stave, the E♭ chord, G(3) - B♭(5) - - E♭(8) in the original key becomes the F major chord A(3) - C(5) - - F(8) in the new key for the first bar of the music. In the second and third bar, the original chord of B♭7, F(5) - A♭(7♭) - B♭(8) - D(3) becomes C7, G(5) - B♭(7♭) - C(8) - E(3) in the new key, before returning to the E♭ chord (original key) and F major (new key) for the fourth bar.

Original key E♭ major

New key F major

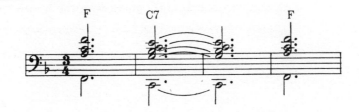

The first four bars in the original key of E♭ major

The transposed four bars in the new key of F major

Continue to transpose "Santa Lucia" from the key of E♭ to the new key of F major. On page 93, your manuscript is ready to use with the key signature and time signature already written in, along with the first four bars above.

If you would like to confirm that you have transposed "Santa Lucia" correctly, turn to the back of the book for the complete arrangement in the new key of F major.

Providing that you follow the sequence of steps for successful transposition you should now be able to transpose between any keys of music. You may find that accidental sharpened and flattened notes take on another form in being transposed, ie. a sharp (♯) in one key may be a natural note in another key etc. You will soon hear if any notes need adjusting when you play the music through.

Transpose some of your favourite arrangements. You will feel a great sense of achievement.

SANTA LUCIA
IN THE KEY OF E♭ MAJOR

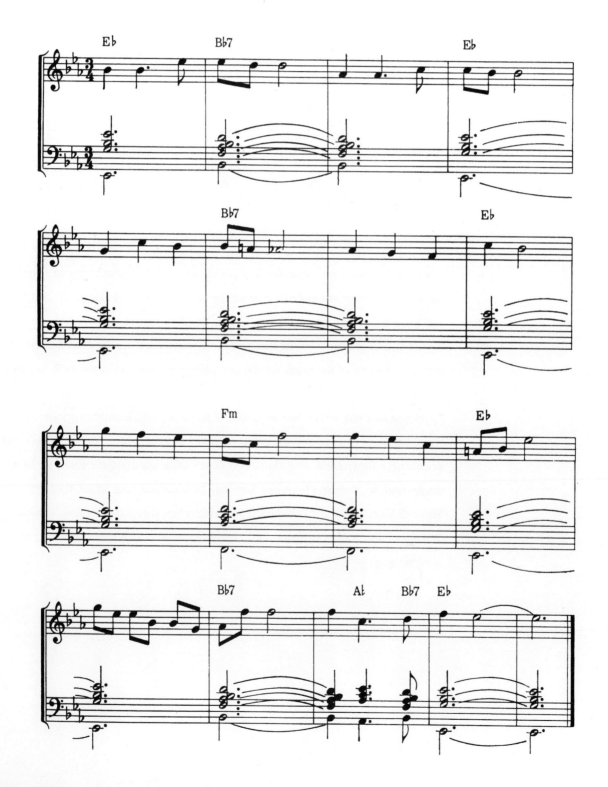

For reference:

1	2	3	4	5	6	7	8
E♭	F	G	A♭	B♭	C	D	E♭
F	G	A	B♭	C	D	E	F

SANTA LUCIA
IN THE KEY OF F MAJOR

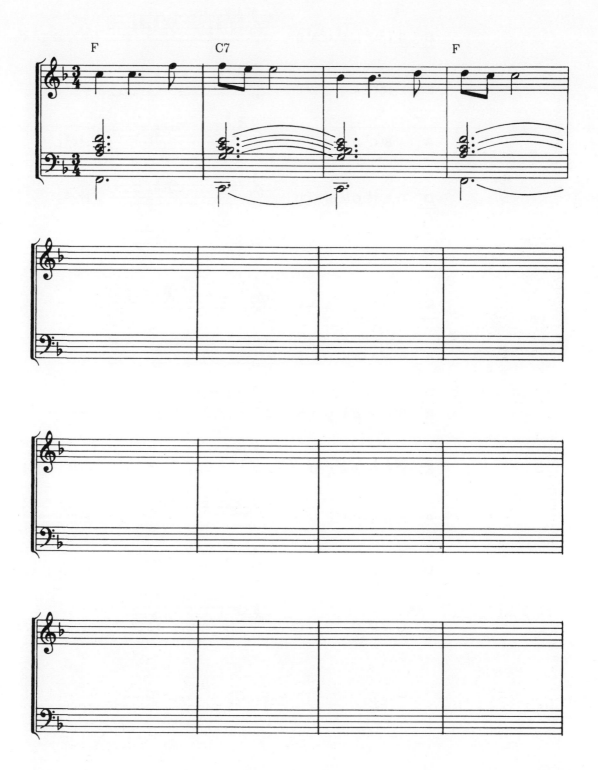

■ THE MUSICAL LADDER

The following illustration of major scales, keys of music and their key signatures will be used for reference in the subjects discussed in the following sections of this book.

KEY	Major scales	Key signatures	
F♯	F♯ G♯ A♯ B C♯ D♯ E♯ F♯		F♯ C♯ G♯ D♯ A♯ E♯
B	B C♯ D♯ E F♯ G♯ A♯ B		F♯ C♯ G♯ D♯ A♯
E	E F♯ G♯ A B C♯ D♯ E		F♯ C♯ G♯ D♯
A	A B C♯ D E F♯ G♯ A		F♯ C♯ G♯
D	D E F♯ G A B C♯ D		F♯ C♯
G	G A B C D E F♯ G		F♯
C	C D E F G A B C		
F	F G A B♭ C D E F		B♭
B♭	B♭ C D E♭ F G A B♭		B♭ E♭
E♭	E♭ F G A♭ B♭ C D E♭		B♭ E♭ A♭
A♭	A♭ B♭ C D♭ E♭ F G A♭		B♭ E♭ A♭ D♭
D♭	D♭ E♭ F G♭ A♭ B♭ C D♭		B♭ E♭ A♭ D♭ G♭
G♭	G♭ A♭ B♭ C♭ D♭ E♭ F G♭		B♭ E♭ A♭ D♭ G♭ C♭

Having learnt how to transpose music into various keys, the next step is to join two different keys together by composing a 'modulation'. Modulation is the musical term for a smooth movement in harmony from one key to another, comprising bars of music containing a left hand chord progression formed from the Musical Ladder. The harmony of the seventh and minor seventh chords, already established in Part II are ideal for modulation. To refresh your memory, chord progressions such as Am7 to Dm7 to G7 to C etc. are formed upon the keynotes of the Musical Ladder and progress in a downward movement on each step.

When you have transposed the music, the bars of the modulation will be formed between the last chord of the original key and the first chord of the new key. The two arrangements should have the same time signature which must be maintained for the modulating bars.

There are two steps to modulation:

1. identify the two home keynotes on the ladder which represent the two keys of music to be joined together

2. form seventh or minor seventh chords upon each keynote of the ladder until reaching the keynote representing the new key. You can choose the number of bars for the modulation between 1 and 4 and this will determine how many keynotes are used, one keynote chord for each bar of music.

To compose the first modulation I will use the two arrangements of "Plaisir D'Amour" with their identical time signatures. I have chosen three bars for the modulation, requiring three chords which will be formed between the last chord of C major in the first arrangement and the first chord of E♭ major in the transposed arrangement.

Refer to the ladder to identify the two home keynotes of C to represent the original key of C major and the keynote of E♭ representing the new key of E♭ major. The seventh and minor seventh chords of the modulation will be formed on the three keynotes of C, F and B♭, preceding the keynote of E♭.

Original keynote	C
	F
	B♭
New keynote	E♭

The second of the last two bars in the original key can become the first bar of the modulation by adapting the C chord to Cm7, or C7, to start the chord progression.

Moving one step down on the ladder, form an Fm7 or F7 chord on this keynote, followed by a further step down to form a B♭7 chord only on the B♭ keynote to lead into the first chord of E♭ in the new key.

Example 1

Last chord of original keynote

C	becomes C7 or Cm7
F	becomes Fm7 or F7
B♭	becomes B♭7 only

First chord of new keynote   E♭   major

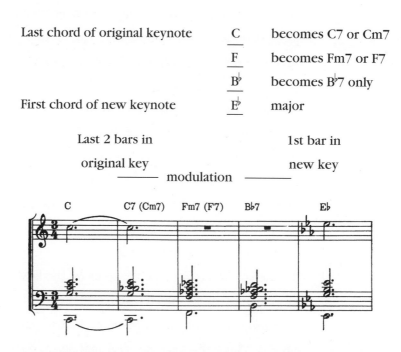

Play left hand chords and bass pedals only while maintaining the timing ¾ for the modulating bars.

Play example 2 of the last four bars of "Plaisir D'Amour" in the key of C major, followed by the three modulating bars and the first four bars in the new key of E♭ major, creating a smooth movement in harmony between the two keys of music.

Example 2

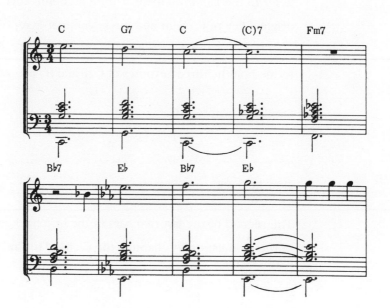

Advanced chords can be played as an alternative to the basic chords in the previous illustration, while the keynote sequence of the ladder for forming and naming the left hand chords remains unchanged. Adapt the first modulating chord of C major to C9, followed by the F9 and B$^\flat$13(9) chord as substitutes for the Cm7, Fm7 and B$^\flat$7 chords (see example 3).

In the inversions of the C9 and F9 chords, the uppermost note of G in each chord will be played outside the octave F to F on the lower manual so that the F9 chord is played in the nearest position to the B$^\flat$13(9) chord to achieve smooth movement.

Example 3

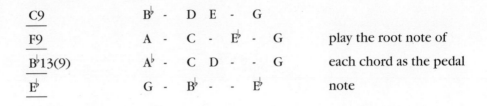

C9	B$^\flat$ - D E - G	
F9	A - C - E$^\flat$ - G	play the root note of
B$^\flat$13(9)	A$^\flat$ - C D - - G	each chord as the pedal
E$^\flat$	G - B$^\flat$ - - E$^\flat$	note

last 2 bars   modulation   1st bars new key

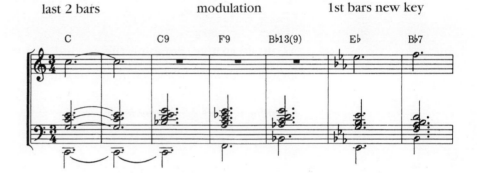

If you are joining together two keys of music which are represented on two adjacent keynotes of the ladder, modulation is very simple, ie. you have transposed music from the key of C major into the key of F major and a one bar modulation is composed by adding the seventh note of B$^\flat$ to the last chord of C in the original key (C7) to move smoothly into the first chord of F major in the new key.

C   last chord of the original key

C7   modulating chord

F   first chord of new key

adjacent keynotes	modulation movement
C	C
F	(C7)
	F

Example 4 illustrates the last bar in the key of C major, one modulating bar containing the C7 chord and the first bar in the new key of F major.

Example 4 (bass stave)

last bar　　　　　　　　first bar

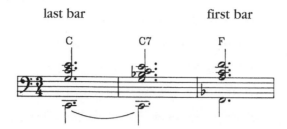

If the last chord of the music is held for two bars the modulation can take place during bar three containing a lead-in note to the new key.

Example 5 Chord held for last two bars (treble stave)

bar1　　　　　　bar2　　　　bar3

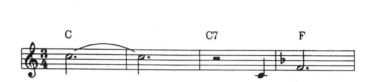

As an alternative, combine the second and third bars of example 5 to include both melody notes with the modulating chord of C7, example 6.

Example 6 Bars 2 & 3 combined

One more example should clarify; to join together the two keys of B♭ and E♭ simply form the B♭7 chord by adding the seventh note of A♭ to the B♭ chord to move smoothly into the E♭ chord.

Example 7 1 bar modulation between the keys of B♭ & E♭

You cannot climb up the ladder in seventh chords to reach a new keynote as the harmony of the seventh chords is achieved by a downward movement on the ladder.

A similar movement to the first modulation can be used even when the new keynote is in a higher position on the ladder than the original keynote, as the modulating chords will again be formed upon the three preceding keynotes to the new keynote, to compose a three bar modulation.

For example, you have transposed music from the key of F major into the key of A major and you would like to compose a three or four bar modulation to join them together. The keynote of A is in a higher position on the ladder than the original keynote of F, so referring to the ladder identify the keynote three steps up from the new keynote of A which is F♯. Move one step at a time down the ladder from F♯ to B to E to the new keynote of A, forming a minor seventh or seventh chord upon each keynote. In example 8, I have chosen the three modulating chords of F♯m7, Bm7 and E7 into the first chord of A in the new key of A major.

Musical Ladder

			key
F♯			F♯
B	chords used for 3 bar modulation		B
			E
E			A
			D
A	new key		G
D			C
			F
G			B♭
			E♭
C			A♭
			D♭
F	original key		G♭

The ending chord of the original key, F or F6, will move smoothly to the first chord modulation F♯m7 with the notes of F♯ - A♮ - C♯ - E moving to the Bm7 chord F♯ - A B - D, followed by the E7 chord G♯ - B - D E into the A major chord (example 8).

Example 8

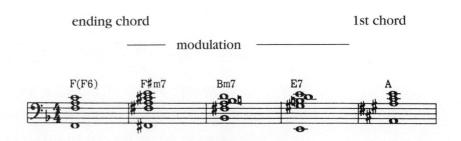

The left hand chord progression and bass pedal notes in the modulations are melodious to listen to without melody notes being played, but if you would like to add them refer to the section below, entitled 'Composing A Melody for the Four Bar Introduction', which can also be used for these modulations.

Advanced chords can be played for the modulation in previous example 8 by forming inversions of the F#m7 (A♮ - C# - E - F#) and Bm7 (A B - D - F#) chords. Substitute the E7(♭9) chord with the notes of G# - B - D - F for the E7 chord followed by the Amaj9 chord (G# - B - C# - E) resolving to A major in the first bar of the new key (example 9).

Example 9

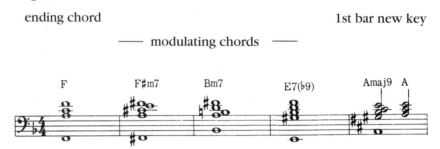

As the F# keynote appears to be the highest point on the ladder, a three bar modulation into the key of B major seems to be impossible. However, the upward keynote sequence of the ladder is formed upon the dominant fifth notes of the scale. If we extend the ladder above the F# keynote the next keynote up will be C#, the dominant fifth note of the F# scale. The dominant fifth note of the C# scale, G#, will be the next keynote up the ladder, and so on.

A three bar modulation is now possible into B major. G#m7 or G#7, C#m7 or C#7 and F#7 only into B. To find these chords more easily, enharmonically, G#m7 is also A♭m7 (G# pedal) and C#m7 is also D♭m7 (C# pedal) (example 10).

Example 10

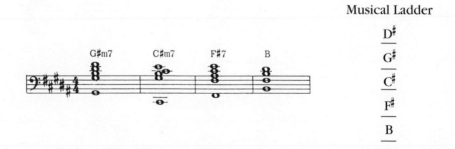

You should now be able to join together any two keys of music without sitting at the manual, as you can simply write the modulating chords directly from the ladder on to your manuscript after deciding how many bars you are going to compose. Later, you may be able to memorise the ladder well enough to turn the pages of a music book and play each arrangement, one after the other, with modulating chords between them.

As an alternative to using the ladder, if you are familiar with the notes which make up a chord, you can look at the manual to play a chromatic modulation when each note of each left hand chord moves by a semitone distance.

To form a chromatic modulation between the keys of C and E♭ major play the chords of C, B, B♭, B♭7 into E♭.

I have already established in Part II that the seventh chord moves in harmony to the major chord, so by adding the seventh note to the B♭ chord (B♭7) the otherwise lengthy movement is shortened.

Chromatic modulation	C	chord -	G - - C - E
	B	chord -	F♯ - - B - D♯
	B♭	chord -	F - - B♭ - D
	B♭7	chord -	F - A♭ B♭ - D
	E♭	chord -	G - B♭ - - E♭

Each note of each chord moves by a semitone distance until reaching the B♭7 chord which leads smoothly into the E♭ major chord. Whole tone movement between the chords, when each chord moves by a tone distance at a time, can complete the previous modulation in only two steps between C and E♭. The C major chord moves tonally to the B♭ chord, before forming the B♭7 chord, by adding the A♭ note to complete the movement into the E♭ chord.

Modulating in this way, between the key of F major and the key of A major, the tonal movement of the left hand chords is F - E♭ - D♭ - C♭ (B) into A major, with minor seventh and seventh chords (example 11).

Example 11 Tonal modulation between the keys of F & A major

Key of F major   modulating chords   key of A major

To simplify this form of modulation, the tonal movement will depend upon identifying tone distances on the organ manual to form chords upon them. Each tone distance will name the chord to be played.

Initially, chord progressions accompanied by the bass pedal notes create adequate harmony to be played on their own, but later you can add a melody line for the modulating bars. Composing a melody is discussed in the next section.

Treble stave to accompany example 11

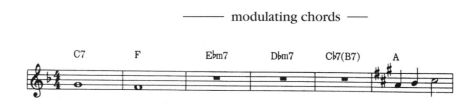

─── modulating chords ───

C7   F   E♭m7   D♭m7   C♭7(B7)   A

INTRODUCTIONS TO MUSIC

As very few arrangements are musically introduced to the listener, I will now show you how to compose your own introductions. These will comprise bars of music which create an impression of the music to follow. This form of embellishment is ideal for middle-of-the-road and standard music.

The Musical Ladder and left hand chord progressions will again be used for forming an introduction to music. The bass pedals and left hand chords only can be adequate, but melody notes can be included. Either way, the introduction will prepare the listener for the music they are about to hear.

An introduction, normally of four bars duration, is formed in a similar way to a modulation. The chords will again follow in harmony with seventh and minor seventh chords leading into the first bar of the music, as did the modulation, with the exception of the first bar of the introduction, which will contain the first chord written in the music. So, music written in the key of C major will normally start on the chord of C major. This C chord will be used as the first chord in the first bar of the four bar introduction and will be known as the home key chord.

1st bar containing the home key chord of C

Home key chord   1st chord of music

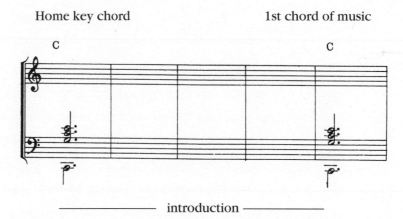

─────── introduction ───────

To compose the second, third and fourth bars, the left hand chords will be formed upon the three preceding keynotes on the ladder to the home keynote, representing the key of music to be introduced.

So, there are four steps for composing an introduction:

1. prepare two staves of manuscript as treble and bass and divide into five bars. Identify the home keynote on the ladder to represent the key you are introducing. Insert the key signature and time signature on the manuscript, before writing the home key chord above the first bar of the introduction.

2. ascend in one leap three steps up the ladder from the home keynote to form a minor seventh, or seventh chord upon this keynote for the second bar of the introduction.

3. descend one step down the ladder to form a minor seventh or seventh chord upon this keynote for the third bar of the introduction.

4. descend one further step down the ladder to form a seventh chord only at this stage upon this keynote for the fourth bar of the introduction which will lead you into the first chord of the music.

The timing of the music must be maintained for the introduction bars.

So, to compose a basic four bar introduction to the key of C major, first prepare the manuscript, then in bar 1 insert the home key chord of C, as in the previous illustration. Bar 2, ascend three steps up the ladder in one leap to the keynote of A to form an Am7 or A7 chord upon this keynote. Bar 3, descend one step to the keynote of D to form a Dm7 or D7 chord upon this keynote. Bar 4, descend one step to the keynote of G to form a G7 chord only on this keynote to lead into the home key chord of C major in the fifth bar.

Example 1   4 bar introduction into C major

Musical Ladder

     key

     $\underline{F^\sharp}$

     $\underline{B}$

     $\underline{E}$

     $\underline{A}$ A(m7 or 7)   head for home

     $\underline{D}$ D(m7 or 7)   forming 7th or m7th

     $\underline{G}$ G(7)   chords on each step

     $\underline{C}$ C home key chord   of the ladder.

     $\underline{F}$

     $\underline{B^\flat}$ Home is the key the music is written in.

     $\underline{E^\flat}$

     $\underline{A^\flat}$

     $\underline{D^\flat}$

     $\underline{G^\flat}$

Example 2 uses the minor seventh chords for the second and third bars, and the G7 chord for the fourth bar of the introduction.

Example 2

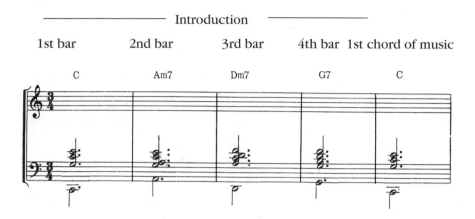

The chords of Am7 or Dm7 in the second and third bars can be substituted by the A7 or D7 chords. It will be a personal choice, although the minor seventh chords can be more suitable for the sweeter types of music such as ballads, waltzes etc., while the seventh chords are ideal for introducing the faster 'up-tempo' music such as quicksteps for dancing.

Play example 3 below to hear the variation of harmony created by the substitution of seventh chords.

Example 3

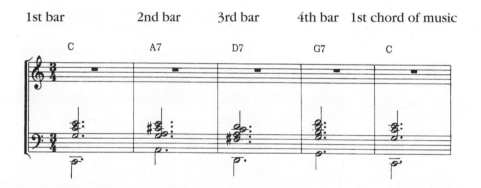

Refer to the Musical Ladder on page 103 to see the formation and sequence of chords for a four bar introduction to the key of C major.

The rule is now established for forming a four bar introduction to any key of music using basic chords and bass pedal only. To take another example, for a basic four bar introduction to the key of E♭ major you must first prepare the manuscript and identify the home keynote of E♭ on the ladder. Bar 1, insert the home key chord of E♭. Bar 2, ascend three steps up the ladder in one leap to the keynote of C to form a Cm7 or C7 chord upon this keynote. Bar 3, descend one step to the keynote of F to form an Fm7 or F7 chord upon this keynote. Bar 4, descend one step to the keynote of B♭ to form a B♭7 chord only upon this keynote to lead into the home key chord of E♭ major.

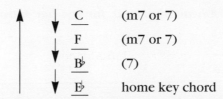

C	(m7 or 7)
F	(m7 or 7)
B♭	(7)
E♭	home key chord

Example 4 uses minor seventh chords for the second and third bars and the B♭7 chord for the fourth bar of the introduction.

Example 4

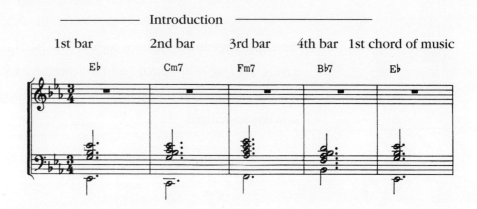

The chords of Cm7 or F7 in the second and third bars can be substituted by the C7 or F7 chords.

Advanced chords can be played as an alternative to the basic minor seventh and seventh chords in a four bar introduction, providing that the sequence of keynote names remain the same.

Example 2, the home key chord of C major can be adapted to Cmaj9 (G - B - D E) followed by A9 (G - B C♯ - E), D9 (F♯ - A - C - E) and G13 (♭9) (F - A♭ B - - E) leading directly into the home key chord of C major. The keynote sequence of the ladder A - D - G - C is unchanged.

A	(9)
D	(9)
G	(13(♭9))
C	home key chord

The name of each advanced chord, C, A, D and G, must be played as the pedal note, as it is not included in the chord.

Example 5 *Advanced chords for a 4 bar introduction into the key of C major*

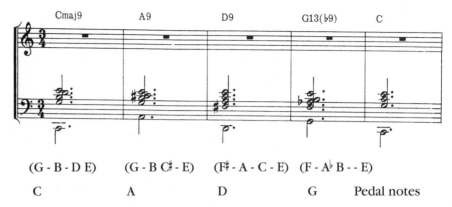

Advanced chords can be used for the four bar introduction to the key of E♭ major, starting with E♭maj9 and followed by C9, F9 and B♭13(♭9) before leading into the home key chord of E♭. The keynote sequence on the ladder remains unchanged.

Example 6 *Advanced chords for a 4 bar introduction into the key of E♭ major*

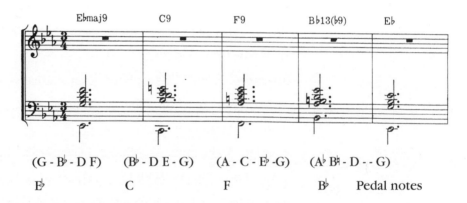

■ USING DIMINISHED & AUGMENTED SEVENTH CHORDS IN AN INTRODUCTION

A diminished seventh chord can be substituted for the chord in the second bar of a four bar introduction. In the second and third illustration, the chord in the second bar can be played as a C diminished seventh chord, rather than A7 or Am7. When the home keynote chord on the ladder is used for two out of four bars, ascend only two steps of the ladder to start forming the chord for the third and fourth bars of the introduction.

Example 1: playing in the key of C major, the home keynote of C is used for the first and second bars (C) and (Cdim7) chords, followed by the normal progression of Dm7 and G7 chords in the third and fourth bars.

Example 2: playing in the key of E♭ major, the home keynote of E♭ is used for bars one and two (E♭) and (E♭dim7), followed by the normal progression of Fm7 and B♭7 chords, in the third and fourth bars.

	Bar 1	Bar 2	Bar 3	Bar 4	Home key chord
Example 1					
Home key C major	C	Cdim7	Dm7	G7	C
Example 2					
Home key E♭ major	E♭	E♭dim7	Fm7	B♭7	E♭

The basic G7 and B♭7 chords in the fourth bar of example 1 and example 2 could alternatively be played as augmented seventh chords. The sequence of chords will then be C - Cdim7 - Dm7 - G7aug - C in the first example, and E♭ - E♭dim7 - Fm7 - B♭7aug - E♭ in the second example.

Another alternative is to play the seventh chords with a flattened ninth note. The G7 chord could be played as G7(♭9) and the B♭7 chord could be played as B♭7(♭9).

Remember to use the inversions of the chords if, in their playing position, they are not close enough to the next chord of the music to ensure smooth chord changing.

You should now be able to compose a four bar introduction into any key of your choice. You will need to visualise the home key opposite any keynote to proceed to introduce your favourite music. But while the left hand chords and bass pedals are adequate for the introductions, composing a melody will complete these embellishments.

■ COMPOSING A MELODY FOR THE FOUR BAR INTRODUCTIONS

Each bar of a melody must contain notes, or rests, to the value of the beats in a bar according to the time signature of the music.

Initially, one note from the left hand chord is sufficient. This single melody note can be played in one or more bars of the music, providing that the note is included in each of the left hand chords.

In example 2 on page 104, a single melody note of C could be played for the first, second and third bars, as the note is included in each of the chords of C, Am7 and Dm7, but in the fourth bar of the introduction the note of C is not included in the chord of G7, so one of the notes from the chord (G - B - D - F) must be played instead.

To avoid a large gap between the melody notes, the note of B rather than the note of D or F from the G7 chord is chosen to precede the lead-in note of G in the fourth bar of example 1.

Example 1

If you are adding a melody line to example 3, page 104 the melody note for the second bar will not be C natural, but C#, because of the C# note in the A7 chord. However, the C natural melody note can be played with the D7 chord once again in the third bar, as it is a note of a chord.

Now choose one note from each left hand chord for each bar. The C note will still be played for the first bar, the E note for the second bar, followed by the D note in the third bar before playing the fourth bar as written in the previous example, keeping the melody notes close together (example 2).

Example 2

Using melody notes other than those in the left hand chord often produces a discordant sound. For simplicity, the melody notes duplicated from the left hand chords will be classed as 'important' notes and any notes inserted between the important notes will be called 'passing' notes to be played as a means of reaching an important one.

Play a C or C6 chord (G - - C - E) or (G A - C - E) to hear the agreement of sound by duplicating their notes as the melody notes. Still holding the C or C6 chord, play the 'passing' notes of B, D and F to hear how they do not agree with the left hand chords.

Example 3

important notes   passing notes

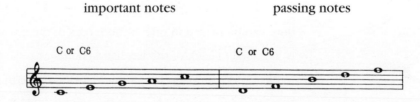

Play example 4 to hear each important note from the left hand chord in each bar.

Example 4 Important notes from each left hand chord in agreement of sound

E G C E   G A C E   F A C D   G   B D

Passing notes are really notes of scale played between important notes which are essential to harmony. When passing notes are added between the important notes of the previous illustration, you will hear how they need to pass onto an important note. The passing notes are marked with a star in example 5.

Example 5 Passing notes included in each bar

The passing notes marked x in the previous illustration are:

bar 1 - B & D (not in C major chord)

bar 2 - B & D (not in Am7 chord)

bar 3 - B & E (not in Dm7 chord)

bar 4 - A & C (not in G7 chord)

The six quaver notes in each bar are solely for the purpose of highlighting the sound of passing notes when played between important notes and will not create an effective four bar introduction.

The E♭ melody note is one of the important notes in the chords of E♭, Cm7 and Fm7 in the first three bars of the following illustration. In the fourth bar, the E♭ note can be a passing note to the important note of D in the B♭7 chord, while the third note of C in the same bar is also a passing note to the important note of B♭ (example 6).

Example 6

Now play each important note from each left hand chord in each bar in example 7.

Example 7 Identical melody notes & notes of each left hand chord in
each bar

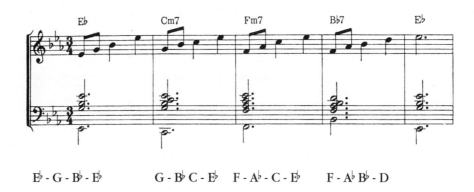

E♭ - G - B♭ - E♭   G - B♭ C - E♭   F - A♭ - C - E♭   F - A♭ B♭ - D

Example 8 Now add the passing notes between the important notes.

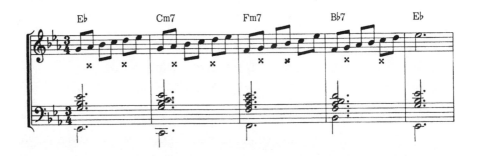

The passing notes marked x in the previous illustration are:

bar 1 - A♭ & D (not in E♭ chord)

bar 2 - A♭ & D (not in Cm7 chord)

bar 3 - G & B♭ (not in Fm7 chord)

bar 4 - G & C (not in B♭7 chord)

The simple rules have been established for composing a complete four bar introduction into the two keys of C and E♭ major. Experiment with your own music to compose introductions to them, following the same method. Paste your instructions to your music, above the treble stave at the beginning of each arrangement.

■ COMPOSING AN ENDING

Music is written like the phrases and sentences of a letter and left hand chord progressions are arranged to blend in harmony to create these musical phrases and sentences. I have shown you, throughout Part III, how chord progressions are used in this way. This last chapter will be devoted to embellishing the ending of an arrangement.

Understanding the keynote sequence of the Musical Ladder will help you recognise the endings to phrases or sentences in the music.

I briefly mentioned in the section on modulation that, when ascending the Musical Ladder, the sequence of keynotes is formed upon the dominant fifth notes of scale, ie. one step up the ladder from the keynote of C (1), first note of the C major scale, is the keynote of G (5) dominant fifth note of the C major scale. One more step up the ladder from the keynote of G (1) is the keynote of D (5), dominant fifth note of the G major scale etc.

D major scale		D	e	f♯	g	A
		1				5
G major scale	G a b	c	D			
	1		5			
C major scale						
C d e f G						
1	5					

```
A
─
D
─
G
─
C
```

The dominant fifth note of one major scale is also the first note of another major scale.

Descending the Musical Ladder, the sequence of keynotes is formed upon subdominant fourth notes of scale, ie. one step down the ladder from the keynote of C (1), first note of the C major scale is the keynote of F (4), subdominant fourth note of the C major scale. One more step down from the keynote of F (1), first note of the F major scale, is the keynote of B♭, subdominant fourth note of the F major scale etc.

C major scale	C d e	F				
	1	4				
F major scale		F	g	a	B♭	
		1			4	
B♭ major scale					B♭	c d E♭
					1	4

```
C
─
F
─
B♭
─
E♭
```

The subdominant fourth note of one major scale is also the first note of another major scale.

A cadence is an ending and appears in three forms in music: perfect, plagal and imperfect. A perfect cadence of a seventh chord, followed by a major chord has appeared regularly in the subjects in this book. This ending is known as 'five to one' in music theory, as the seventh chord is formed upon the dominant fifth note of scale (5) and is followed by the major chord, formed upon the tonic (root or 1st) note of scale (1), (5) to (1).

ie. G7 (5) is followed by C major (1)

    B♭ (5) is followed by E♭ major (1)

The two keynotes upon which each chord was formed are on adjacent steps of the Musical Ladder. The chord formed upon the upper keynote with a seventh note added, moves down one step to the next keynote to form the perfect cadence, or ending (5 to 1):

$$\downarrow \quad \frac{G(5)}{C(1)} \quad \downarrow \quad \frac{G7}{C} \qquad\qquad \downarrow \quad \frac{B♭(5)}{E♭(1)} \quad \downarrow \quad \frac{B♭7}{E♭}$$

A plagal cadence will use a major chord formed upon the subdominant fourth note, followed by a major chord formed upon the tonic note. Now the order is reversed and the major chord of the lower keynote of two on the ladder moves up the ladder to the next keynote to play a major chord on the tonic (4 to 1):

ie. F major chord moves up to the C major chord

$$\uparrow \quad \frac{C(1)}{F(4)}$$

The imperfect cadence, also called a 'half close', suggests that although the chords of the music indicate the end of a phrase, there is more to follow. The two simplest chord formations to give this effect are: 1. a major chord on the tonic keynote followed by a major chord on the dominant fifth keynote (1 to 5); 2. a major chord on the subdominant fourth keynote followed by a major chord on the dominant fifth keynote (4 to 5).

ie. 1. C major to G major   2. F major to G major

$$\uparrow \quad \frac{G(5)}{C(1)} \qquad\qquad \uparrow \quad \frac{\frac{G(5)}{C}}{F(4)}$$

Most music will end on a major, or sixth chord. We can now use the ladder to embellish and extend a simple ending by identifying the home keynote on the ladder as the home key chord (as in the introduction section above) and moving one step down the ladder to the subdominant fourth note to form a major, sixth or minor sixth chord upon this keynote, then moving back to the home key chord to play it as a major or sixth chord.

In the key of C major, the last chord is usually C major (home key chord). Identify the keynote of C on the ladder, move one step down to form an F major, F6 or Fm6 chord, before moving back to the home keynote chord of C or C6.

Ladder:

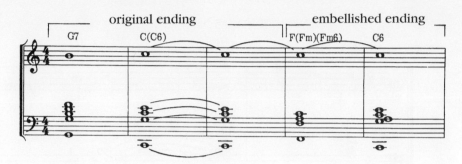

The melody note of C in the last two bars of the original ending can be sustained for the extended ending as it occurs in each of the left hand chords.

As a final example, playing in the key of E♭ major, the final chord is E♭, which you will identify on the ladder as the home keynote. After this chord has been played, move one step down the ladder to the keynote of A♭ to form the chord of A♭, A♭6 or A♭m6, before returning to the home key chord of E♭ or E♭6 to end the music.

Extended ending to the key of E♭ major

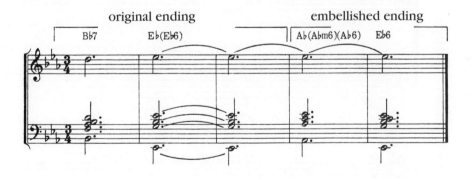

SANTA LUCIA
IN THE KEY OF F MAJOR